How to be an
Ethical Shopper

About the author

Melissa Corkhill, writer, mother of two and editor of The Green Parent magazine is passionate about green issues.

With a background in media, Melissa launched the UK's leading green lifestyle magazine five years ago. It can be found in stores across the UK and is also available in the US and Canada and covers all aspects of green living. Find out more at www.thegreenparent.co.uk.

Melissa believes in raising awareness so that parents can make informed choices about their family's health and wellbeing. Her work has been described as "inspiring, strong and beautiful."

I dedicate this book to my family

HOW TO BE AN
ETHICAL
SHOPPER

The practical guide to buying what you believe in

How to be an Ethical Shopper

ISBN 978 1904601 456

First published in Great Britain in 2007 by Impact Publishing Ltd.
12 Pierrepont Street, Bath, BA1 1LA
info@impactpublishing.co.uk
www.impactpublishing.co.uk

A Cataloguing in Publication record for this title is available from the British Library.
Credits: Photo credits; Impact Publishing Ltd.

Printing (sheet-fed litho)
Printed in the UK by **Cambrian Printers**, Aberystwyth who hold ISO14001 certification for environmental management (Certificate No. E00564). Inks are vegetable-based, water and solvents recycled. Files were transferred electronically with plates made direct from print resolution PDFs supplied by the publisher.

Paper
Printed on an uncoated, elemental-chlorine-free stock (text - Edixion Offset; cover - Challenger Laser Matt). The merchant and mill are ISO14001 and EMAS (Environmental Management System) accredited with pulp sourced from managed and sustainable forests.

CONTENTS

Introduction

Choosing ethically produced goods from socially responsible companies can have an incredible benefit for our planet and fellow human beings. This book highlights the choices we make in every area of daily life, aiming to make the life of an ethical shopper a much easier and more pleasant one.

Sometimes shopping ethically can be a bit confusing. For example, is it better to choose fairtrade or organic? This book looks at all the options and the labels and helps you to make the most responsible decision in every situation.

What's inside?

The book is divided into three sections; first we look at what ethical consumerism means and why it is important. In this section you will find information about the labels and grading on everyday products, how to recognise them and what they mean.

In section two you will find everything from cars to toys and how to shop ethically for each and every purchase. All aspects of daily life are dealt with from food to clothes, travel to tourism, money to entertainment. In each case the best ethical choices and shopping tips are given.

Section three is there for those of you looking to step off – it offers some of the alternatives to consumerism including trading schemes and the trend for reducing and re-using goods.

At the back of the book the **resources section** enables you to delve deeper into the fascinating topic of ethical consumerism.

I hope that this guide provides a useful starting point for effecting positive change in your life today. Never underestimate the power of the individual and remember Mahatma Gandhi's wise words: "Be the change you want to see in the world."

Melissa Corkhill

1

What is ethical consumerism?

Why be an ethical consumer?

It is important for us to consider how and where we spend our money because we are plundering our planet's natural resources at an alarming rate. Increasing levels of carbon emissions are responsible for global warming and climate chaos, which, if allowed to continue at current levels, spell death and destruction for millions of people, not to mention animal and plant species. If we wish to have any future, we need to stop consuming with such wanton abandon. We need to consider the social and environmental impact of each purchase we make. And we need to do this for ourselves, not just for the health of the planet. Scientists are no longer arguing about whether climate change exists, they are starting to look for ways in which we can reverse the devastation that we have created with our love of fast cars, big houses and foreign travel.

This book aims to give you, the reader, some of the tools necessary to make the right choices. The green industry is growing and there are many more alternatives available now than there were several years ago. Think of eco fashion, which has taken off over the last year, with ethical boutiques popping up around the country, beautiful stylish clothes made from hemp, organic cotton, recycled materials and even bamboo. It is now possible to dress head to toe in gorgeous eco-clothes that turn heads without resorting to attire created in sweatshops in the developing world under appalling working conditions. We can choose the most energy efficient appliances from fridges to washing machines according to an eco-rating. Holidays are available that support responsible tourism and that don't add to the devastation of natural areas as many package holidays do. You can even go ethical in your sleep with natural and organic mattresses available, beds made from reclaimed wood and organic cotton sheets. And if all this luxury sounds cost prohibitive, have a look inside to

find out how ethical consumerism doesn't have to cost the earth. How to be an Ethical Shopper leads you through what could be a minefield, highlighting the good, the bad and the ugly.

In today's climate it is better for us to think carefully before buying and adding to the over-consumption that is already rife in our society. But spending wisely and with conscience is also a useful tool for the ethical consumer. Ethical shopping means choosing goods that cause less harm to the environment, humans or other creatures. It means choosing those products that have a positive social and environmental impact. Using this book you can find out what the ethics behind your regular purchases are and use this information to shop ethically.

So how did we get here?

Our history of over-consumption goes back to the 1950s when after the Second World War, industry was booming again and companies were looking to sell more goods. Used to decades of scrimping and saving shoppers weren't consuming at high enough levels, so marketing and ad men were brought in to sell the nation a dream. A dream of more stuff, bigger, better cars, larger, more modern homes, filled with better, more technologically advanced equipment.

11

Obsolescence was born, the concept that when a product was old, outdated or broken it could be replaced by a newer model. This drive was supported by television and now we live in a culture where the majority of us work increasingly long hours to finance a lifestyle we're not sure we want any more. If you are feeling disillusioned, there are ideas in section three on how to consume less. Shopping with a conscience is another way to stop feeling guilty and start putting your money where your mouth is.

Fairtrade

Enter a high street shop and every item on sale has a hidden story. A fashionable shirt could weave a sorry tale of an underage worker in Bangladesh forced to work a 20 hour day and sleep on the floor beside her sewing machine for around 50p per day. Every item from clothing to flowers tells a tale. The tale of freshly cut flowers available at supermarkets and garages is an especially troubling one. They are often grown on South African farms, staffed mainly by women, many of whom suffer respiratory diseases and skin conditions due to the chemical cocktail sprayed on the plants to keep them in optimum condition. Or take the £3 jeans sitting pretty in the aisle next to the groceries at the supermarket. At this price, is it really feasible that the factory worker responsible for making them was paid a fair wage? All too often these stories can seem far removed from our lives in the West. What can we possibly do to help those in developing countries who suffer such crushing working conditions?

We can start shopping with a conscience, and question the stories behind our favourite brands and products. If trade secrets behind the big brand products on the shelves were laid bare we would most likely think twice before buying them. Every time we choose to buy a cheap top or smart trainers we are also making the choice to support the corporation behind it, and in turn the company's ethics. So it is wise to know what those ethics are before getting out our wallets.

FAIRTRADE

Guarantees
a **better deal**
for Third World
Producers

Basically if we pay less than the real costs for an item of clothing, piece of fruit, packet of coffee then someone else has to foot the bill. More often than not, it is the impoverished producer and the environment that suffer the consequences but neither can sustain this level of exploitation forever. Sooner or later consumer capitalism will be responsible for its own bills. And in the meantime, fair trade is not just a pipe dream but rather a viable alternative that has been working around the world for decades.

What is Fairtrade?

Fairtrade is about better prices, decent working conditions, local sustainability, and fair terms of trade for farmers and workers in the developing world. By requiring companies to pay above market prices, Fairtrade addresses the injustices of conventional trade, which traditionally discriminates against the poorest, weakest producers. It enables them to improve their lot and have more control over their lives.

Serious efforts are being made to introduce fairness into international trade. Around 40 years ago the first fairly traded products became available in the UK. In 1974, Tearcraft launched with the sale of Bangladeshi jute from a basement flat in Newcastle. Oxfam followed in 1975 with its Helping through Selling campaign, offering fairly traded goods made by skilled craftsmen from developing countries to consumers in the UK. In 1994 the Fairtrade Mark was launched and over ten years later can now be found on 2000 + products.

Controlled by the Fairtrade Foundation, consumers will find the Mark on food products from fresh fruit to rice, and other goods from footballs to knickers. This helps ethical shoppers recognise goods that ensure a fair price and fair working conditions for their producers.

Fairtrade products tend to cost slightly more than their mainstream counterparts. Whilst corporations compete against each other for consumer money and for market share they also have a common interest in keeping production costs as low as possible and therefore enhancing profit margins. As Fairtrade grows and takes control of these margins from the large multinationals, the greater the difference will remain with producers and will eradicate the fairtrade premium.

What does Fairtrade mean for third world producers?

There are an estimated one million farmers and workers directly involved in Fairtrade. In addition, millions more people benefit indirectly from the investments in communities. It means better terms of trade and decent production conditions. The Fairtrade Foundation, with its partners, maintains these standards by regularly inspecting developing world suppliers, and checking contracts and trade terms.

What is the difference between 'fair trade' and ethical trading?

Ethical trading means companies are involved in a process of trying to ensure that the basic labour rights of the employees of their third world suppliers are respected. The Fairtrade Mark, which applies to products rather than companies, aims to give disadvantaged small producers more control over their own lives. It addresses the injustice of low prices by guaranteeing that producers receive fair terms of trade and fair prices – however unfair the conventional market is.

Is Fairtrade a subsidy that encourages farmers to grow more coffee and therefore contribute to global oversupply and low prices?

"No," says the Fairtrade Foundation, "subsidies are government payments which lower the price of goods with the intention of encouraging their production and/or consumption or of making them more competitive than imported goods. The cost of these subsidies is borne by taxpayers or consumers.

Fairtrade, on the other hand, is a voluntary model of trade that brings consumers and companies together to offer small-scale farmers a price for their coffee that covers the cost of production and provides a sustainable livelihood so that they can send their kids to school and pay their bills."

Oversupply is usually a result of coffee growers increasing production in the brief periods when prices are high. However, it is clear that the recent surge in global coffee production, and consequent low prices, is largely a result of government agricultural export policies in Vietnam and large-scale farm expansion in Brazil. Paradoxically, in an attempt to compensate for lower prices, many small-scale farmers dependent on coffee will increase output at the expense of quality.

But paying a higher Fairtrade price need not increase production; rather, it gives farmers other options – to invest in quality improvements and gain access to speciality markets or diversify into other crops to reduce their dependence on coffee.

How to recognise an ethical product

Labelling has become more prolific in recent years making it easier to choose ethically. We look at some of the labels that you might find on products from food to fridges below. As the green industry has grown, many companies are publishing information about their ethical stance on their websites and a number of useful guides are available to download from standard agencies. These are mentioned throughout the book under the relevant sections.

Labels are there to help make our shopping decisions easier but in actual fact with the plethora of different labels now shown on packing it can be a very confusing affair indeed. Here we showcase some of the most widely used ethical labels and grading systems:

RECYCLING

The Mobius Loop

The internationally recognised recycling symbol is the 3 chasing arrows icon. Each arrow represents an aspect of a successful recycling programme: collection, remanufacturing/reprocessing into a new product, and finally purchase by the consumer.

Green Dot

A registered trademark that means that a financial contribution has been paid to an authorized packaging recovery scheme. Can be found on packaging and ensures that the manufacturer has considered the end-of-life disposal of the product.
www.pro-e.org

HOUSEHOLD

VOC Label

This label indicates the relative content of VOCs (Volatile Organic Compounds) in paints and associated products. VOCs cause air pollution and are detrimental to human health. Non-toxic paints are often called Low-VOC, No-VOC, VOC-Free, odourless, odour-free and green, natural or organic paints. Look for these to ensure least harm to the environment and your family's health. **www.coatings.org.uk**

Oeko-Tex Standard 100

An international certification system for textiles garments covering all stages of production. Labelled products are tested by independent institutes for an extensive range of harmful substances based on the latest scientific findings and legal regulations. All parts of labelled articles must meet the defined requirements. Visit **www.oeko-tex.com** for more information about the latest research in this area.

The European Eco-Label

Award of this label signals that the item meets 'rigorous environmental criteria and proper fitness of use', but it does not necessarily mean that a product contains any recycled content. Products featuring the Eco-label should become more widespread as manufacturers apply to be allowed to use the label on products that comply with the appropriate criteria, which are based on detailed life cycle analysis.

Some countries also have national schemes like the **Nordic Swan** in Scandinavia and the **Blue Angel** in Germany. These labels can be found on goods in Europe that meet high environmental standards such as natural paints. For more about ecolabels visit the network of the **Global Ecolabelling Network** at **www.gen.gr.jp**

The **Rainforest Alliance** works with foresters, farmers and tour operators to ensure that their goods and services are environmentally and socially responsible. Its certified seal of approval appears on products including timber, paper, bananas and coffee which have been grown or made sustainably. **www.rainforest-alliance.org**

The **FICGB (Forestry Industry Committee of Great Britain)** Woodmark is used to indicate to timber specifiers and consumers that a wood product is derived from British grown timber, which has been felled in accordance with a standard defined by regulations implemented by the Forestry Authority. This means a lower environmental impact as the wood has not been air freighted to Britain and therefore has a smaller carbon footprint.

The EC Energy Label

By law, the **EC Energy Label** must be displayed on all white goods such as fridges, freezers and washing machines. The label also provides an assessment of the product's energy efficiency, as well as giving an estimate of electricity and water consumption on standard settings, performance, noise levels and whether the product has gained an ecolabel. The label identifies the most energy efficient models on a scale of A-G, A being the most efficient.

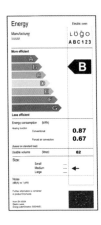

Energy Star

The **Energy Star** logo means that the energy consumption of a product is below an agreed level, when in 'stand-by' mode. The logo appears on some types of office equipment, such as computers, monitors, printers and fax machines. Within the EU the Energy Star is a voluntary labelling scheme. **www.energystar.gov**.

The **Energy Efficiency** logo has been introduced by the Energy Savings Trust, an independent government funded body, to identify products and services, which save or use less energy. This label is used to promote energy saving appliances.

The **Trademark of the Forest Stewardship Council (FSC)** indicates that the wood used to make the product comes from a forest that is well managed according to strict environmental, social and economic standards. The forest of origin will have been independently inspected and evaluated according to the principles and criteria for forest management. **www.fsc-uk.org**

The **PEFC Council** (Programme for the Endorsement of Forest Certification) is an independent organisation whose logo provides an assurance that its certified wood and paper products have been independently audited as coming from sustainably managed forests. **www.pefc.org**

FOOD

The **LEAF Marque** is about linking environment and farming. It is one of the approaches to farm management that gives you, the consumer, the choice of buying affordable food produced by farmers who are committed to improving the environment for the benefit of wildlife and the countryside.

The **Marine Stewardship Council** rewards environmentally responsible fisheries management and practices with its fish logo. It enables consumers to choose products that come from well-managed fisheries and have not contributed to the environmental problem of overfishing. **www.msc.org**

GENERAL

The **Soil Association** Organic Symbol is the UK's most recognisable trademark for organic produce. When used on food packaging, it tells the consumer that product is certified to the highest organic standards and provides reassurance of organic authenticity. Farmers, growers, processors and retailers value the Organic Symbol as it embodies high professional standards of production, handling, storage and sale. **www.soilassociation.org**

Fairtrade Mark

The **Fairtrade Mark** is a widely recognised label awarded to products that meet international Fairtrade standards. The Fairtrade Foundation operates under the Fairtrade Labelling Organisations International (FLO) to license the use of the Fairtrade Mark in the UK. Fairtrade is not just about ensuring producers get a fair price for their products. There are new environmental standards that must be met too. **www.fairtrade.org.uk**

FAIRTRADE
Guarantees
a **better deal**
for Third World
Producers

20

VEHICLES

The **UK Fuel Economy Label** for all new cars aims to encourage reduced energy consumption and carbon emissions in the transport sector. The label shows how much carbon dioxide a car emits. Carbon dioxide is the main greenhouse gas responsible for climate change. The label gives estimated fuel costs for 12,000 miles and the vehicle excise duty for 12 months so you can see how much these will cost you before you buy. Lower carbon emissions mean lower road tax and lower running costs. It has been introduced voluntarily by the car industry under the auspices of the Low Carbon Vehicle Partnership. **www.lowcvp.org.uk**

Boycotting

What is a boycott?

A boycott happens when a group of consumers choose not to purchase goods from a certain company, usually because of a poor environmental or social record. People power used in this way can be very persuasive.

Successful boycotts include the 1995 Greenpeace action against Shell, protesting about the multinational oil giant's Brent Spa oil platform in the North Sea. The proposed plan to dump the oil storage platform into deep Atlantic waters was met with fierce resistance from environmental activists. Greenpeace mounted a successful boycott of Shell across Northern Europe which damaged profitability and brand image. Several months into the boycott due to falling sales and a drop in share price, Shell withdrew the plan to sink the Brent Spa oil platform. In a well-organised campaign, consumers can change corporate behaviour.

Are they always successful?

Oxfam is concerned that consumer boycotts can sometimes harm the very people that they are trying to protect; workers lives can be put at risk if demand for their goods in the Western world is significantly reduced. To this end it is worthwhile carefully researching who will bear the brunt of boycotting actions and to always accompany with letters/emails to explain to the company in question why you are avoiding their products. Otherwise directors easily write off a drop in sales as just current market conditions. Ethical consumer magazine has a list of current consumer boycotts and consumer action at **www.ethicalconsumer.org**.

Some of the current high profile boycotts include:

De Beers for supporting the Botswana government's efforts to forcibly remove Bushmen from their ancestral lands to resettlement camps.
Contact: **020 7687 8700** or ***www.survival-international.org***

Esso for allegedly sabotaging international action on climate change.
Contact Greenpeace at **020 7865 8100** or visit: ***www.stopesso.com***

Nestlé for its marketing of baby milk formula, which is considered irresponsible and may infringe the International Code of Marketing of Breastmilk Substitutes.
Contact: ***Baby Milk Action, www.babymilkaction.org*** or tel: **01223 464420**

Tesco due to its escalating use of Radio Frequency identification. The tiny computer chips embedded in products or packaging allow monitoring of items which consumers normally consider private, like clothing, wallets and backpacks. Contact **CASPIAN** (Consumers Against Supermarket Privacy Invasion and Numbering) at ***www.boycotttesco.com***

Shop Local

Walking along most British high streets, you could be forgiven for not knowing exactly where you are. As large multinationals have gradually taken over our high street shops, small independents have all too often been priced out, turning our town centres into a homogenised testament to our consumer culture.

So why is it important to favour local independents over large multinationals? In its **Clone Town Britain report** the **New Economics Foundation (NEF)** likened chain stores to economic weeds sucking the life out of our high streets, destroying diversity and killing off real local shops. Retail spaces once home to a thriving mix of independents; bakers, bookshops, butchers, grocers, newsagents and family owned general stores are becoming filled with faceless supermarket retailers, fast-food chains and global fashion outlets.

In February 2005, a **NEF** report stated "Tesco opens one Express store each working day. As they expand small general stores close at the rate of around one

per day." And it's not just the family-owned general stores that are disappearing. Specialist stores such as bakers and fishmongers shut at a rate of 50 per week between 1997 and 2002. This loss of diversity is having a damaging effect on our localised economies in this country. It destroys small businesses and can mean a loss in skilled workers and a greater percentage of the workforce having to settle for McJobs (low paid work that requires few skills and offers few prospects) to support their family. The death of diversity on the high street undermines democracy, attacks our sense of place and belonging and therefore wellbeing. It hands power to an unaccountable corporate elite, ultimately pulling apart the natural system on which our livelihoods and local economy depend.

However there is still time to save our remaining independent towns from turning into clone towns. Find out more at the New Economics Foundation (NEF) website www.neweconomics.org. An independent think tank that believes in economics as if people and planet mattered, **NEF** works on economic, social and environmental issues through research, campaigning and raising awareness through the media. Their current 'hot topics' include real world economics, clone town britain, and well-being. Register your support for their Local Works campaign at **www.localworks.org**

Many shoppers are now choosing to 'Shop Local' and in the process rediscovering great local food, good conversation, friendships and the pleasure of buying from people who have a vested interest in their products and your custom.

2

Ethical Shopping

Clothes, Jewellery and Beauty Products

Clothes

This chapter deals with the clothing industry and the issues behind it such as workers' rights, the environment and animal rights. We look at each area in turn and discover the alternatives available to the ethical shopper. At the end of the chapter we check out the ethics involved in jewellery production and also take a look at the beauty industry.

THE PEOPLE

Cheap Chic

There is a revolution on the UK high street: cheap is the new black. Women's clothing prices have fallen by a third in ten years, and the 'value' end of the market is booming, doubling in size in just five years to snap up £6bn of sales in 2005. We now buy 40% of all our clothes at value retailers, with just 17% of our clothing budget.

As prices fall, consumers have responded by buying more clothes, and by changing the way in which they buy them. Collections used to change just twice a year but the pressure is now on to have something new in store every month, in response to rapidly changing trends. 'Fast fashion' is the new fad, giving shoppers the latest styles just six weeks after they first appeared on the catwalk, at prices that mean they can wear an outfit once or twice and then replace it.

This trend for throwaway fashion has been made possible by the rapid expansion of high street, low value retailers such as Primark and Matalan, and the growth of the supermarket clothing sector. Primark, for example, is a true retail phenomenon. Owned by Associated British Foods, the chain has been valued at £3.1bn. Its profits rose 30% in 2005 off the back of a 17% sales increase (sales were worth over £1bn). Last year, its Managing Director, Arthur Ryan was voted the most influential man in UK fashion.

Meanwhile, supermarkets are keen to expand their non-food offers and gain customers by offering a 'one stop' shopping experience for consumers wanting cheap goods of all kinds.

The fall in clothing prices on the UK high street and supermarket own-brand clothing has been passed on to suppliers. Average garment export prices in China, for example, fell by 30% between 1997 and 2002, at the same time as production costs rose 10%.

Many high street stores claim that they are doing their best to improve working conditions in their supply chains. Evidence from decades of research in the garment industry suggests, however, that the way in which they demand ever lower prices and ever reduced lead times is driving down working conditions from what is already a very poor starting point. It's not just campaigners who say this, but also labour rights auditors, supply chain management consultants, and even some companies.

One key right workers should enjoy is to earn a living wage, defined as enough to meet their basic needs and those of any dependants, plus a small amount of discretionary income. Here is a typical story from the Clean Clothes Campaign about a young woman in a Pakistani factory:

> *"Because of the fact that wages are so low and the cost of living so high, she finds it very hard to make ends meet. At 18, she is the only earning member of her family of three. She is an only child and both her parents are jobless. She spends almost 40% of her income on the rent of her one bedroom house. When told that it is checked [by auditors] that workers should get at least the minimum wage set by the government, which they all do, she said that if they think this wage is enough they should all try to live on this amount for a month and decide if it is OK."*

How can I find out where my clothes are made?

The first thing to do is to trace the label. That little piece of fabric is at least supposed to provide you with all the information you need. Many data-bases can be found on the internet to help research garment companies and determine which brands are owned by which companies.
Try **www.cleanupfashion.co.uk**

A number of initiatives selling clothes that are ethical, organic or fairly traded have sprung up in the wake of the international anti-sweatshop movement, which aim to meet the needs of a rising number of consumers, individuals and institutions, now demanding "clean clothes". The Fairtrade Mark has recently been applied to some cotton products meaning that ethical consumers can now purchase clothes bearing the Mark. See the company profiles throughout this section, and also the resources at the back.

What is a sweatshop?

A sweatshop is a workplace with conditions that do not meet Internationally accepted minimum labour standards.

What is a living wage?

A living wage enables workers to meet their needs for nutritious food and clean water, shelter, clothes, education, health care and transport, as well as allowing for a discretionary income. Workers should earn enough to provide for the basic needs of themselves and their families, to allow them to participate fully in society and live with dignity. Their wages should take into account the cost of living, social security benefits and the relative standards of other groups.

What is a trade union?

An association of employees dedicated to the purpose of improving their working conditions.

What is child-labour?

The employment of children under an age determined by law. This practice is considered exploitative by many countries and international organisations.

www.traid.org.uk

31

THE ENVIRONMENT

According to the Soil Association, the textiles industry is one of the largest polluters in the world. And we need an alternative. One that isn't dangerous and doesn't cause such destruction to our environment. Around a quarter of the world's insecticides are used to grow conventional cotton, and ten percent of its pesticides. At least 8,000 chemicals are used to turn raw material into clothes, towels, bedding and other items that we put next to our skin every day. Shockingly, use of the pesticide endosulfan in farming cotton in developing countries is causing the poisoning of thousands of workers, often resulting in their death. The scientific community's jury is still out on the exact effects to human health of many of the chemicals used in cotton farming, with potential side effects including cancer and disruption to the hormonal and reproductive systems of the body.

Genetic modification

More than 50% of conventional cotton is now believed to be genetically modified. It is a difficult crop, vulnerable to insect attacks, typically grown in vast monocultures and heavily dependent on chemical inputs. GM cotton varieties seek to tackle growers' problems by either making them dependent on a particular herbicide or causing the plants to constantly exude an insect-repellent toxin. This method is likely to kill many beneficial insects as well as harmful ones and as a result of long-term use insects are expected to develop immunity to it, rendering it useless anyway.

It is possible to grow cotton using organic methods, which seek to nurture the soil and the environment instead of relying on destructive chemical inputs. Organic cotton is grown without the use of pesticides and clothes are produced without the use of bleaches, formaldehyde and heavy metal dyes common in standard textile production.

Does growing cotton without chemicals work?

Yes. Organic farmers around the world are showing that there is no need to rely on dangerous chemicals. Black ants keep caterpillars and other pests under control in Uganda. In other countries, mixtures of natural soap, chilli and extracts from local trees are used to repel pests, which can then be eaten by chickens or other birds. Insect traps can be used to detect when levels of infestation are rising, allowing farmers to time their applications to gain the best effect.

Pest, weed and disease control is achieved through crop rotation, choice of varieties, timing of cultivations and habitat management to encourage natural predators. Crop rotation is at the core of organic crop production, providing nutrients to the soil, helping prevent pest, weed and disease problems and maintaining the soil structure.

An answer to chemicals for cotton?

Cotton uses more pesticides than any other crop, including strong carcinogens like organochlorines. Some biotechnologists see Genetic Modification as the solution to this overload of chemicals. Biotech companies such as Monsanto have engineered GM cotton that is resilient to insects. They claim this allows farmers to reduce pesticide use on their crops but greens are concerned that a strain of GM resistant insect will develop and that biodiversity will be affected. Another concern is that we have no information about the implications of releasing GM crops into the environment.

The most ethical textile?

Hemp is one of the purest, most complete plants on Earth. It grows almost anywhere and requires no pesticides or fertiliser. The plant is good both for the soil and the atmosphere. It makes an excellent source of textile and paper. The fibres are long and very strong, and people have been using hemp to make textiles for around 6000 years. The hemp plant grows to heights of 15-20 feet and the fibre, when stripped from the plant, is as long as the plant itself, giving hemp added strength when woven into textile. Discovery of new softening techniques and the investment of millions of dollars into the hemp factories in China has resulted in hemp garments that still retain all the traditional qualities of hemp textile but with a softness and quality that has not been seen before. Hemp Clothing is available from Enamore **www.enamore.co.uk**, THTC **www.thtc.co.uk** and **Yaoh www.yaoh.co.uk**

Bamboo is 100% naturally grown and sustainable. It thrives naturally without using any pesticides or fertilizers and is completely biodegradable. As the fastest growing plant in the world, bamboo grows to its maximum height in about 3 months and reaches maturity in 3-4 years. It spreads rapidly across large areas. Because of this, bamboo is known to improve soil quality in degraded and eroded areas of land. If organic clothing made from bamboo becomes popular, it means more bamboo plantations, which means more photosynthesis and less greenhouse gas. "The greatest challenge facing mankind" would get just a little easier. Bamboo Clothing is available from **www.bambooclothing.co.uk**

Profile: Bishopston Trading

Bishopston Trading (BT) was set up 22 years ago by Carolyn Whitwell to create employment in the impoverished village of K.V.Kuppam in South India which had been linked to Bishopston, Bristol in a friendship link since 1978.

Carolyn says of the UK fashion industry, "I think the overproduction of cheap throwaway clothing not only squeezes the producers but wastes limited resources and creates unbiodegradable rubbish. It also means that people no longer value their clothing or good workmanship. However, at Bishopston, customers have a guarantee that we put the wellbeing of our producers before profit and sell honestly made, good value, attractive fairtrade organic cotton clothing in beautiful colours."

BT are members of IFAT, the shops are members of BAFTS and they are a licencee of the Fairtrade Foundation. Carolyn says, "We have worked with the same suppliers in the same village for 22 years and our two organisations have grown up together – starting with 4 tailors in K.V.Kuppam and 3 employees and one shop in Bristol to our present position with 230 tailors and craftworkers and approximately 250 handloom weavers in K.V.Kuppam and 36 employees of Bishopston Trading Company in UK."

On the future of the fashion industry in the UK, Carolyn says, "It could go either way – maybe more big companies will be forced to abide by the labour laws of the countries they import from – or they will go on importing excessive amounts of ridiculously cheap, badly made clothing from countries too poor to refuse to co-operate. Tesco boasts about making a profit on its £3 jeans; how could producers possibly be paid enough for making them? Meanwhile M&S effectively forces its suppliers to help pay for its advertising – in the last 6 months they have spent £56 million on advertising – think what better things could be done with a sum like that!"

www.bishopstontrading.co.uk

Profile: Chandni Chowk

Paul Garrod, of Chandni Chowk says, "Our first consideration is to produce high quality and individual products. It has always seemed obvious to us that the best way to achieve this is to treat our producers with respect and reward them fairly and promptly. Much of the production is hand skill based using natural fibres and dyestuffs and made by families. The whole throwaway culture is foreign to us. As is the use of petrochemicals to produce fibres and yarns." Members of BAFTS, Chandni Chowk's webshop at **www.chandnichowk.co.uk** offers a wide range of beautiful handmade clothing.

Profile: Adili

Launched in 2006, Adili is based on two core values; respect for people and respect for the environment. Adam Smith, CEO says, "Increasingly we will be looking deeply in to the product story for every line we stock and visiting our suppliers in countries of origin, as well as encouraging them and supporting them to gain certification in terms of Fair Trade, use of organic raw materials and for labour standards. We use an Ethical Trading Consultant to guide us through this 'minefield' and to minimise the risk of compromising the ethics."

In the future Adam hopes to see consumers exercise their purchasing power to move away from fast fashion and 'value' retailers – understanding the consequences for purchasing a £2 t-shirt for example. He hopes that more multiples will follow the lead of Marks & Spencer and move ethical values to the core of their businesses, not just 'jump on the bandwagon'. He would like to witness an upturn in UK clothing manufacturing and to see the strengthening and increasing market share of ethical clothing retailers like Adili. View their range online at **www.adili.com**

Profile: Clothworks

Linda Rowe set up Clothworks in 1997 to offer products that are well designed and ethically produced. "Having been involved in the fashion industry for twenty years, I have watched the industry exploit people from all directions," Linda explains "I feel that this has to stop. And to this end, I have been very involved with 'Ethical Consumerism' since 1990." One of Linda's concerns with the clothing industry today is that too much is being produced and there is no consideration given to durability. "Because of this people often do not value the articles of clothing that they possess." On the other hand, Clothworks offers an assurance that a great deal of thought has gone into the way that the clothes are made. And through using natural fibres and natural dyes the clothes are not having a negative impact on the planet. The cloth used is certified where certification is available. The clothes are made in the UK and also by a fair trade co-op in Brazil. Linda hopes that every part of the industry will be shamed into changing their production practices and that all the independent organisations currently set up to monitor the industry will work together, as she feels there is currently a gulf between the 'Fair trade' and 'Organic' movements. **www.clothworks.co.uk**

www.clothworks.co.uk

Profile: Clean Slate

Clean Slate was founded by husband and wife entrepreneurs, Mark Rogers and Carry Somers. They created the company in March 2006 after searching the UK for cotton school uniforms which were not chemically treated for Carry's daughter, Sienna. Of principal concern to them was the potentially harmful environmental and health effects of PFOA; a compound used to make Teflon which is then applied to mass-produced children's garments for an "Easy-Care" finish. Carry Somers is the owner of Pachacuti who for 14 years has been a retailer and wholesaler of fair trade clothing and accessories from the Andes. Find out more at **www.cleanslateclothing.co.uk**

Profile: Gossypium

When Abi and Thomas Petit set up Gossypium their aim was to demonstrate that it is possible to create products that are socially and environmentally positive. They believe that all production can and should be ethical. All Gossypium products are Fairtrade and Organic certified cotton but their main promise is that they buy direct from the farmers and that their supply chain is transparent. The husband and wife team visit and foster long term relationships with both the farmers and the factories. Abi and Thomas believe that the industry will look very different in 5 years time; that the British consumer will not put up with low quality products once they have been offered an alternative. **www.gossypium.co.uk**

ANIMAL RIGHTS

It takes as many as 40 animals to make just one fur coat. Every year, millions of animals – like coyotes, bobcats, lynxes, otters, foxes, minks and raccoons – are trapped or drowned in the wild and strangled, gassed, or electrocuted on fur farms.

Trappers use painful steel-jaw leghold traps to catch wild animals so that they can be turned into clothing. Animals who are farmed for their fur live in filthy conditions, trapped in cages and fed meat by-products. No law protects these animals, which means that fur farmers can pretty much get away with murder. Remember, fur only looks good on its original owner!

Silk production is a big industry in Asia but unfortunately this natural fabric is not as ethical as it seems. Child labour and poor pay are common in the sericulture industry and the working conditions are often hot and cramped. To produce silk, the cocoons of a silk worm are unravelled; each is up to a kilometre in length. Conventional silk production involves boiling the worm inside the cocoon. Sometimes it is eaten afterwards, otherwise it is thrown away.

What to do:

Choose fairtrade to ensure that you are not supporting child labour in harsh conditions. And it is possible to find spun or wild silk which spares the worms in its production. The cocoons used to produce wild silk are collected from the rainforests and the moths fly free after the silk is collected. Learn more about silk production at **www.bwcindia.org** or **www.vegansociety.co.uk**

Leather is a by-product of the meat industry. The environmental implications are not good; treating a raw hide can use up to 75 litres of water. Mineral tanning uses chromium and is a fairly chemistry-intensive process. The hides are "pickled," raising the pH to a high acidity level to enable chromium tannins to enter the hide. For preservation purposes, fungicides and bactericides are also applied. The alternative, vegetable tanning is slower; chrome tanning takes less than a day and produces a stretchable leather which is preferred for use in handbags and garments. Vegetable tanning uses fewer chemicals in the process. Tannery pollution mainly affects workers in the developing world; 62% of the

2.4 million people in Kasur, Pakistan are suffering from disease caused by industrial waste. And the main contributor to their ill health? Tanneries. Unfortunately there are no standards governing the production of leather so the most ethical option is to avoid it where possible and seek out an alternative. If you must buy leather, go for second-hand and vegetable tanned products.

The alternative?

Vegetarian leather substitutes are often made from plastic such as polyurethane so aren't exactly a green option. Still these are better than leather especially if you are an ethical consumer keen not to support the meat industry.

How to be an ethical shopper: clothes

- Use less – save money and the planet by shopping for clothes far less often

- Rediscover your local charity shop. Close the loop by taking your unwanted clothes to the charity shop, or textile recycling bank

- Read up on the fashion industry and its human rights issues

- Look for the Fairtrade mark on clothing products

- Choose organic cotton to reduce pesticide usage and to avoid genetically modified cotton

- Talk to your favourite stores and brands – write letters asking them to improve their ethical stance

- Shop with small independent ethical companies as found in our resources section

- Avoid fur

- Get creative – try making your own, take up knitting or sewing and see what you can create yourself.

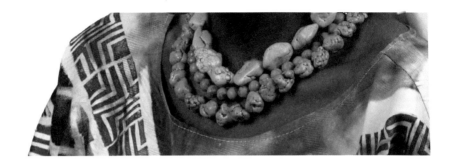

Jewellery

The issue surrounding the ethics of the jewellery industry are deep and conflict-ridden.

The production of jewellery has been blamed for widespread child labour, dangerous working conditions, environmental degradation and wars.

Cheaper jewellery is often produced in Asian sweatshops and there have been reports of migrant workers in China suffering from dust lung in the jewellery production factories. They are left crippled by the disease caused by cutting semi-precious stones and setting into jewellery for Western markets. Again, sadly, child labour is common.

How to be an ethical shopper: Jewellery

- Choose fairtrade jewellery. Try People Tree **www.ptree.co.uk**, Adili **www.adili.com** and Cred **www.cred.tv**

- Ask for reassurance from your local jeweller that their diamonds are not from conflict zones. See **www.conflictdiamonds.com**

- Coral jewellery is an environmental no-go. Reefs are one of the world's most fragile ecosystems, already under threat from agricultural effluent and global warming

- Precious stones often come from small-scale mines, which provide work but in dangerous conditions. Choose fairtrade if possible.

Health and Beauty

The main concerns surrounding the health and beauty industry are animal welfare and the toxins used in products, although there are also human rights issues in some of the larger factories. In terms of health, a study at Lund University in Sweden found that female hairdressers were a third more likely to give birth to babies with serious physical defects. Repeated exposure to toxins in products such as hairspray and dyes appears to be the culprit. And according to Alicia Di Rado at the University of California, "Studies suggest that those who have worked for 10 or more years as a hair stylist could have a risk of bladder cancer five times that of the general population."

Many environmentalists are also concerned about deforestation and extinction of plant species. Palm oil for example is widely used in the cosmetic industry and to make soaps. Although there are some areas of sustainable palm oil production, the vast majority of production causes widespread deforestation of rainforest and the displacement of many species including the endangered orangutangs. Read more at **www.palmoil.org.uk**

Petroleum based chemicals such as parabens and Sodium Lauryl Sulphate are found in the majority of toiletries and cosmetics. Giving most products a longer shelf life, lipstick the stay put factor, and sun cream its smooth absorbency, these petrochemicals have revolutionised the beauty industry but at what cost to our health and that of the planet? Skin is the largest organ and the body's first line of defence. It absorbs the products that we put on it and these synthetic chemicals have been detected in human body fluids and body fat. In a random check, the Women's Environmental Network (WEN) found preservatives suspected of mimicking the female hormone oestrogen, in 57% of beauty products. This is especially worrying for women when lifetime increased exposure to oestrogen is linked to a heightened risk of breast cancer. Download Getting Lippy, Cosmetics, Toiletries and the environment from **www.wen.org.uk**.

In addition to the unknown health effects of the chemical cocktail contained in many beauty products, these substances also affect the environment when they are washed down the drain into our water system. Build up of chemicals in our seas and rivers is responsible for gender-bending effects on fish and damage to

marine ecosystems. The packaging is also an issue where cosmetics and toiletries are concerned. Often produced from PVC, a petrochemical that releases dioxins during its production, the plastic containers are difficult to recycle so end up in landfill, where hormone-disrupting chemicals can leach out. Choose glass bottles where possible.

Animal testing

Thanks to heavy campaign work animal testing in the cosmetics industry has been reduced dramatically over the last two decades. The UK has banned all animal testing on cosmetics and their ingredients. However as many of the beauty products sold in this country are imports the ban does not mean that our shelves are free from animal tested products. Animal rights activists claim that around 40,000 animals in Europe and one million globally are subjected to tests every year. Meanwhile consumer surveys show that nearly all shoppers want testing of cosmetics on animals stopped completely. But these same consumers carry on buying the products and supporting the companies responsible for animal testing. If you would like to find out how clean and caring your favourite

brands are visit: **www.buav.org**, home to the British Union for the Abolition of Vivisection where you can find a list of approved companies or order a free copy of their *Little Book of Cruelty-Free*.

BUAV says, "Ethical consumers are in a powerful position to influence the policies and practices of companies that still test on animals. By boycotting animal testers and choosing instead to only buy products that are not tested on animals, conscientious shoppers really can get their message across."

It recommends that you "be an ethical consumer by leaving animal tested products on the shelves and only choosing 'cruelty-free' products instead. There is an ever-growing range of cosmetics and toiletries produced by companies who do not test on animals.

There are loads of different cruelty-free product claims and shopping guides out there but beware, many can be misleading. The only 'not tested on animals' list to trust is the BUAV's ever popular Little Book of Cruelty-Free. This pocket-sized Little Book of Cruelty-Free only lists companies approved by the internationally recognised Humane Cosmetics Standard (HCS)."

How to be an ethical shopper: health and beauty

- Take a closer look at your favourite brands to find out what their ethical stance is

- If you are not happy with it, lobby them by writing letters and pressing for change

- Support ethical businesses such as Essential Care, Green People, Neal's Yard, Spiezia Organics and Weleda or smaller cottage scale industries; Akamuti and Barefoot Herbs. See resources section for contact details

- Look for paraben and SLS free products

- Avoid PVC packaging – choose glass instead and ask your retailer for a refilling facility

- Try making your own beauty products using nature's bounty. Search for recipes online.

Food and drink

Food

Fruit and vegetables are around 30% more expensive in supermarkets than in street markets (*source: Sustain* **www.sustainweb.org**).

Around 60 years ago the majority of our food was local and unprocessed. Advances in communications and transport have changed that and globalisation means that we can now outsource processing and packaging to countries where the pound is strong and human rights records weak. Supply chains that transport our food from the field to the plate have lengthened and become much more complicated.

Food makes the largest single contribution to our ecological footprint. Nowadays most of our food travels long distances before it reaches our plates. Perishable food is increasingly transported by plane, and even food grown in the UK may travel from the farm to a processor, to a wholesaler, then to a central distributor before coming back to the local supermarket. A huge amount of energy goes into the packaging and processing of food and waste is created in its disposal. Yet more energy is required for the production of pesticides and fertilisers, used to grow much of the food consumed in the UK.

Food miles

The distance food travels from where it is produced to where it is eaten – 'from plough to plate' – is often a large part of the environmental impact of food production. The Women's Environmental Network (WEN) estimates that a quarter of the UK's carbon dioxide (CO2) emissions come from transporting food from growers, via processors and distributors, to shops and into our homes. Imports account for 95% of fruit and half of all vegetables consumed in the UK. The average distance we drive to shop for food is also increasing each year.

Joanna Blythman, author of *Shopped* has coined the term Permanent Global Summer Time (PGST) to describe supermarkets stocking food throughout the year, most of which has been flown in from a warmer climate. One study found that a local apple from a village shop travelled 38 miles before reaching the proverbial plate, a British apple bought from a supermarket travelled 223 miles and a New Zealand apple bought in a British supermarket travelled 11,326 miles. This global marketplace present in our supermarkets in the UK, as well as being responsible for huge emissions, is also responsible for the decline in traditional British fare. We have lost two thirds of our apple orchards since 1970 whilst the apples available on the supermarket shelves bear labels from as far afield as New Zealand. Eating seasonally and locally would have a number of knock on benefits; improvements to health, better local economy and less airfreight.

Processing and Packaging

The WEN estimate that processed food requires around 15 times more energy to produce than raw, unprocessed food. Highly processed and packaged 'convenience' foods also contribute to food miles, as each ingredient is transported to various parts of the country for processing and preparation before eventually ending up on your plate. A 'ready' meal will have travelled many more miles than an identical meal prepared at home.

Food packaging accounts for about a third of all household waste in the UK. It is estimated that we spend up to £15 billion on food packaging every year. However, we can choose foods with less packaging and even leave unnecessary wrapping at the till to push the message that shoppers are not happy about the needless overuse of plastic cartons and wrappers on our food.

Pesticides and fertilisers

The production of non-organic food requires more energy, due to the use of articificial fertilisers and pesticides. There is also the health risk of pesticide exposure for producers and consumers.

Organic food

Organic farming severely restricts the use of artificial chemical fertilisers and pesticides, which pollute water courses and damage the soil. Organic farmers fertilise their fields by rotating their crops, using composted manure, and planting crops that naturally feed nitrogen to the soil. Animals are also reared without the routine use of drugs, antibiotics and wormers common in intensive livestock farming. Organic farming is better for the soil, wildlife and animal welfare. Locally produced organic produce is often cheaper than supermarket produce. The Soil Association's organic directory gives details of UK vegetable box schemes. See **www.whyorganic.org**.

The UK is the world's third largest market for organic food topped only by the US and Germany. Spending was over £1 billion on organic food in 2003. This means the growth of food without the use of pesticides and other potentially harmful chemicals, in harmony with our natural environment. There are now 10 organic certification bodies in the UK and around 40 farmers convert to organic every month. Around 70% of organic products carry the Soil Association logo. More info at **www.soilassociation.org**.

Why choose organic?

Better for Animal Welfare

Better conditions, fewer drugs for animals, which are fed on non-GM feed. See Compassion in World Farming at **www.ciwf.org.uk**

Better for Health

This is a hotly debated topic. The Food Standards Agency claims that organic food is "not any safer or more nutritious than conventionally produced food." However, the fact that over three quarters of parents now feed their children some organic food is testimony to the fact that as consumers we believe that it is better for us and our growing children. And surely all those pesticide residues on conventional fruit and veg can't actually be good for you?!

Better for environment

Organic production allows for greater biodiversity and fewer pesticides are required. However 56% of organic food sold in the UK has been imported from abroad. We need to support British organic farmers by shopping at farmers' markets and via farm gate sales to encourage more conversion of agricultural land in the UK to organic farming methods.

Meat

860 million animals are reared every year for their meat. The Consumer Analysis Group recently revealed that the average Briton will eat 760 chickens, 20 pigs, 29 sheep, 5 cows and half a trawler net of fish in a lifetime.

The vast consumption of animal products doesn't come without its own pitfalls in terms of overall health, environmental and animal welfare issues.

Rising meat consumption is putting unsustainable pressure on the earth's land and water resources. Animals need much more water than grain to produce the same amount of food. In addition, land cleared for pasture or to grow crops for animal feed leads to deforestation. In Brazil around 12 million acres of forest have been cut down to grow soya beans for European animal fodder. Methane from cattle is also contributing to climate change.

Our favoured form of protein in Western countries is high in saturated fat leading to greater risk of coronary heart disease and obesity; the latter is in turn linked to 5% of all cancers. These health issues obviously impact upon the already over-burdened National Health Service.

The majority of meat that we eat is intensively reared which can mean animals kept indoors in cramped unnatural conditions, in a bid to increase yields by

unscrupulous farmers. Animals are routinely fed antibiotics and hormone disrupting drugs to promote growth. These substances then end up in the food chain and have been linked to gender bending tendencies in other species. No research has been conclusive about the effect on humans but could partly explain the fact that puberty is occurring earlier and earlier in young people.

Maintaining the fivefold increase in meat consumption that has occurred over the last fifty years worldwide has had a devastating environmental impact. Crops to feed animals are grown with pesticides, fertilisers and GM technology. Livestock account for 10% of greenhouse gases and 13 billion tonnes of farm waste, such as ammonia nitrate, yearly, which can pollute soil and water.

BSE, Foot and Mouth disease and Avian Flu should act as a warning to us of some of the dangers of intensive livestock production. However, some good has come out of these crises, with sales of organic meat growing by over 50% during the foot and mouth epidemic. Whilst sales of organic meat have grown it is unfortunate that much of this demand is met through imports. Supermarkets tend to favour meat from overseas for cost reasons. And the organic standards are not always as stringent as in the UK, for example, in Denmark; free-range pigs can be classified as organic just because they are fed organic feed.

We have lost touch with our meat in the same way that this has occurred with the rest of the food that we purchase. Flesh now comes neatly packaged in polystyrene trays, rinsed in chlorine and bound with plastic wrapping.

How to be an ethical shopper: meat

- Buy and eat less meat
- Choose organic, and locally reared if possible
- Try your local farmers market and butchers to find out the provenance of your meal
- Find out more about vegetarianism.

Fishy business

So, with the maligned meat industry, is fish the answer to provide for our high protein dietary requirements? It seems not. Fears of over fishing, high mercury levels in swordfish and tuna and fish farms being responsible for polluting toxins in our water system mean that this may not be the solution.

In addition, depletion of fish stocks is a two-pronged affair. Over fishing and dwindling plankton levels due to global warming mean that cod larvae, for example, have less chance of survival now than they did ten years ago. Many don't even reach maturity because of the demands of the fishing industry.

So how can you choose ethically?

A campaign group that aims to promote the use of fish from sustainable stock and humane fishing practices, The Marine Conservation Society (MCS) has a Fish to Eat and a Fish to Avoid list on their Fish Online website at **www.fishon-line.org**. Alternatively visitors can order a free copy of the Pocket Guide to Good Fish. Watch out also for their logo, the blue tick mark that denotes fish from well-managed sources.

Different types of fish:

Salmon

The high fat content of salmon makes it susceptible to build up of toxins in its fatty tissues. Farmed salmon, which has a higher fat content than wild salmon is even more at risk. FoE Scotland reported in 2001 that a typical salmon farm uses around 25 chemicals, including dyes to make the fish appear pinker. Opt for wild or organic farmed salmon.

Cod

On fish farms, cod are bred in submerged cages. In the wild they can live for up to 40 years and grow to 6 feet in length but 90% of those caught in the North Sea in 2003 were under two years old and had not yet had a chance to breed meaning that the cod population has taken a severe battering. Avoid cod and **choose an alternative such as pollock, whiting, lemon sole and megrim sole for your Friday night fish and chip suppers**. Grilled or pan fried herring, mackerel, grey mullet and John Dory also provide good alternatives.

Tuna

According to the MCS all commercially fished species of tuna are now listed as endangered. In addition to this, nets are often used that can trap and kill dolphins. Although many brands now carry a dolphin-friendly label on their tins, it's not as simple as that. Unfortunately, research has shown that the reason why dolphin populations haven't recovered is because dolphin calves get caught in the dragstream of the tuna fishing vessels, get separated from their mothers and often die.

Prawns

Fishing for wild prawns can destroy natural habitats and kill other marine wildlife that gets caught in the nets and thrown back dead. It is also possible to buy farmed prawns although harsh chemicals and fertilisers are routinely used in their growth. Waste from the aquaculture industry is dumped in the sea and reports have shown contamination of local water supplies. Save the Children and Oxfam are concerned by reports of child labour and poor pay in India. The farmed variety are usually labelled as King or Tiger prawns. So if you have a soft spot for them, search out organic or Madagascan Tiger prawns. Madagascar is working towards making all its prawn fisheries sustainable and is a better choice than other countries. The report, *'Smash and Grab; Conflict, Corruption, and Human Rights Abuses in the Shrimp Farming Industry'*, is published by the Environmental Justice Foundation and concerned consumers can download a copy at **www.ejfoundation.org**.

Dairy

Modern dairy farming is an intensive industry. To produce maximum milk yields, dairy cows are pushed to their physiological limits through a combination of selective breeding, high-protein feeds, and the latest technology. Along with the production of pigs, chickens and eggs, milk production has become just another factory farm operation.

Specialist breeds of dairy cow suited to local conditions have largely disappeared from our countryside. The high yielding and highly bred Holstein-Friesian, the ubiquitous black and white cow, now makes up 90% of the European's dairy herd. Herd sizes have increased as dairy production has become concentrated on fewer and fewer farms.

Milk yields have increased dramatically. In the 1940's, cows were producing an average of 3,000 litres of milk per cow per year. By 1983/84, average milk yields had increased to 4,940 litres, and by 1995, over 6,300 litres per cow per year were being achieved. The strain of higher milk yield can lead to serious welfare problems such as increased mastitis, lameness, and infertility. And over the years, the average milking life of a cow has steadily decreased; the natural lifespan could be 25 years but today most dairy cows are sent for slaughter at about 5 years old, after only three or four lactations. For more of the key issues within the UK dairy industry such as BSE, transportation and the closely linked veal industry see **www.vegansociety.com**. Conscious consumers can choose organic but some of the concerns remain the same as conventional dairy farming, such as continual pregnancies, unwanted offspring to keep the mother in milk and the inhumane slaughter methods.

Vegetarianism

Five percent of the population in the UK are vegetarian, whilst 1 billion people worldwide eat no meat. Research by the World Cancer Research Fund has shown that vegetarians have lower mortality rates, as well as lower risk of heart disease, obesity and cancers.

Liz O'Neill at the Vegetarian Society says, "Whether your priority is animal welfare, climate change or your own spiritual wellbeing, vegetarianism is a positive choice for anyone seeking to live an ethical lifestyle. To kill an animal just because you like the taste of its flesh is straightforwardly wrong for many people, but even if you have no problem with the idea of slaughter, the meat industry is responsible for an extraordinary amount of damage to our natural environment and vegetarians simply have a smaller ecological footprint. We don't need to eat meat to stay healthy, or to enjoy the best gourmet food around, so if you want to make a change for the better, go vegetarian today." Find out more and download free resources for new veggies at **www.vegsoc.org** or tel: 0161 925 2000.

Veganism

In addition to the ethical reasons for choosing not to eat meat or dairy products, or indeed any products from animals, there are also environmental incentives. Agriculture in general is one of the most resource-intensive and environmentally damaging aspects of industrialised living. What this means for us as individuals is that if we are trying to reduce our car use, limit the amount of water we waste, become more 'energy-efficient' and generally lessen our environmental impact, then we should also examine our eating habits.

People are increasingly becoming aware of the direct correlation between what they eat every day and the health of the planet. Environmentally conscious consumers are concerned not only with food miles, over-packaging, pesticide use and GM foods, but also question the environmental sustainability of modern animal husbandry. Farmers used to be seen as 'custodians' of the countryside,' but the overriding image of modern industrial farming is one of destruction and waste.

World meat production has quadrupled in the past 50 years and livestock now outnumber people by more than 3 to 1. In other words, the livestock population is expanding at a faster rate than the human population.

The raising of livestock takes up more than two-thirds of agricultural land, and one third of the total land area. And these animals are fed with grains and cereals that could have been directly consumed by humans or were grown on land that could have been used to grow food rather than feed. The developing world's undernourished millions are now in direct competition with the developed world's livestock – and they are losing.

In 1900 just over 10% of the total grain grown worldwide was fed to animals; by 1950 this figure had risen to over 20%; by the late 1990s it stood at around 45%. Now, over 60% of US grain is fed to livestock. This use of the world's grain

harvest would be acceptable in terms of world food production if it were not for the fact that meat and dairy production is a notoriously inefficient use of energy. All animals use the energy they get from food to move around, keep warm and perform their day to day bodily functions. This means that only a percentage of the energy that farmed animals obtain from plant foods is converted into meat or dairy products.

Quite simply, we do not have enough land to feed everyone on an animal-based diet. So while 840 million people do not have enough food to live normal lives, we continue to waste two-thirds of agricultural land by obtaining only a small fraction of its potential calorific value.

Obviously access to food is an extremely complex issue and there are no easy answers. However, the fact remains that the world's population is increasing and viable agricultural land is diminishing. If we are to avoid future global food scarcity we must find sustainable ways of using our natural resource base. Industrial livestock production is unsustainable and unjustifiable. Switching to a plant-based vegan diet will not 'save the world,' but it is a significant step towards limiting your individual impact on our increasingly fragile environment.

What is veganism?

The word vegan was first used by Donald Watson in November 1944. In the first edition of 'The Vegan News' Donald stated, "The unquestionable cruelty associated with the production of dairy produce has made it clear that lacto-vegetarianism is but a half-way house between flesh eating and a truly humane, civilised diet." Of course people followed a vegan diet prior to this date; our very early ancestors lived by gathering plant materials before they learnt to hunt. Today there are vegans all over the world with about 250,000 in the UK. At the heart of the vegan lifestyle is compassion. Compassion for people, animals and the environment, which creates a better world for all. A well-balanced wholefood vegan diet meets the recommendations for a healthy diet; reducing the risk of heart disease, some cancers, diabetes and obesity. And when people are healthier there is less of a strain on the health service and they get to enjoy life more. See **www.vegansociety.com** to find out more.

Fairtrade

There will always be some goods you can't source locally, for example, coffee and tea. If this is the case, try to buy initially from your own area, then country and if all else fails to buy fairly traded and organic goods. The Fairtrade mark guarantees a fair price and better working conditions for the producer.

Many farmers in developing countries have to contend with fluctuating prices that may not even cover what it costs to produce their crop. So Fairtrade promises a stable price which covers their production costs, along with a premium that their organisation will be able to reinvest either in the business or local community schemes.

Fairtrade is an alternative approach to conventional international trade. It is a trading partnership which aims at sustainable development for excluded and disadvantaged producers. It seeks to do this by providing better trading conditions, by awareness raising and by campaigning. Consumers can now find everything from fresh fruit to juice, coffee to chocolate that bears the Fairtrade Mark.

FAIRTRADE
Guarantees
a **better deal**

Coffee facts

The collapse of world coffee prices is contributing to societal meltdowns affecting an estimated 125 million people (Source: Wall Street Journal – 8 July 2002).

At the end of the 1980s coffee-exporting nations received $10 billion (33%) of a $30 billion annual retail market. The latest estimates indicate the global coffee market is around $55 billion with exporting countries receiving less than $8 billion (approx. 15%). (Source: International Coffee Organisation 2001).

The top 5 companies (Nestlé, Kraft, Sara Lee, Procter & Gamble and Tchibo) buy almost half the world's coffee beans each year (Source: Oxfam's "Mugged: Poverty in Your Coffee Cup" Report 2002).

For the average non-Fairtrade jar of instant coffee, farmers only receive around 11p* (5%) of the price you pay in shops (*Based on an average 100g jar RRP of £2.14). (Source: Oxfam's "Mugged: Poverty in Your Coffee Cup" Report 2002).

In contrast, for Cafédirect 5065, farmers receive 52p (over 20%) of the price you pay in the shops. (Source: Cafédirect).

Coffee farmers capture only a fraction of the value of production – they receive less than 1% of the average retail price of coffee sold in a coffee bar (Source: Oxfam's "Mugged: Poverty in Your Coffee Cup" Report 2002).

Sales of Fairtrade coffee have doubled in 2 years with one in five cups of filter coffee drunk in the UK now being supplied from a "fair" source. (Source: The Independent, June 2006).

Coffee is the second most traded commodity in the world after petroleum. Of the £35bn the global coffee market represents, £3.8bn accounts for the value of the raw coffee beans traded annually.

PROFILE: Cafédirect

Cafédirect's products are about enhancing the quality of life of the communities who grow them, as much as the enjoyment of those drinking them. They invest in long-term partnerships with farmers to create quality products and the whole product range is Fairtrade. The company works with 35 producer organisations representing the farmers in 11 countries, paying a fair price guaranteed to exceed the cost of production to ensure that over a quarter of a million growers and their families received a decent income. The Cafédirect business model is unique: it ensures the company's 100% Fairtrade commitments exceed the minimum requirements laid down by the Fairtrade Labelling Organisation International (FLO). In fact they have gone beyond Fairtrade with the Cafédirect Gold Standard, a commitment to coffee and tea growers, with a support and development programme and a guarantee that the price paid for the coffee is always higher than the world market price. The Gold Standard enables Cafédirect to form partnerships with growers based on trust, transparency and long term relationships. It strengthens grower organisations, empowering them to trade more successfully. The company's trading policies also aim to contribute to sustainable agriculture and minimise damage to the environment. **www.cafedirect.co.uk**

LOCAL FOOD:

The Farmers' Market

According to recent research 32% of people in the UK visit a farmers' market every year, that's 20 million of us choosing to shop locally at markets dedicated to farm produce. And this really is local shopping, with a limit of 30 mile radius for sourcing produce imposed on most markets around the country.

What is a farmers' market?

A market in which farmers, growers or producers from a defined local area are present in person to sell their own produce, direct to the public. All products sold

66

should have been grown, reared, caught, brewed, pickled, baked, smoked or processed by the stallholder.

FARMA, the National Farmers' Retail & Markets Association independently assesses and certifies farmers' markets round the country to make sure they're the 'real deal' so you can be confident you are buying the freshest, most local produce possible, supporting your local community and economy, and helping the environment by reducing food-miles. Look out for the certification logo.

Gareth Jones at FARMA says that the winter months are not necessarily that lean. "We do have what's known as a hungry-gap in the UK, which starts in early spring. After the cold weather of the winter, there is less produce available but visitors to the markets will still find greens, potatoes, meat, fish and many locally crafted products." When asked about his favourite farmers' market, Gareth says, "It's always the one I visited last, so in this case, the market in The Mumbles at Penclawdd which had a real community atmosphere." His local market in Winchester is a much larger affair, with some 100 stallholders and 10,000 visitors every Sunday. Find your nearest one at **www.farmersmarkets.net**

Profile: Big Barn

Big Barn is a local food website, helping people to find good accountable food through local sources. Anthony Davison, founder says "We believe there are significant problems in the UK food industry. We see a trend towards the separation of producer from customer, where the market is controlled by big business, retailers and middle-men. Where farmers, on average, only receive 9p in every £1 spent on food in a supermarket and where chicken farmers now rear chickens so intensively, to meet low price points, that they contain nearly a pint of bad fat, get hock burns from standing in their own excrement and grow so quickly that their bones can be minced up to make hot dogs. We want to reverse that trend." And customers can register their interest in changing the face of the food industry at **www.bigbarn.co.uk**, where they will receive a fortnightly newsletter full of local food news and the chance to shop locally on the net.

Why do ethical consumers shop at farmers' markets?

Because they benefit:

• Producers

They cut out the middleman allowing increased financial returns through direct selling, price control, and a regular cash flow.

They provide the producer with direct customer feedback on produce and prices.

Transport and packaging requirements are less thus reducing the producers' costs.

They provide a secure and regular market outlet. This is especially valuable for; new producers, producers in organic conversion, and small scale producers who are unable to produce the quantity required by supermarkets.

With the increase in market numbers it is possible for individual producers to attend a substantial number of different markets. A number of farmers have indicated that this form of marketing has helped them avoid bankruptcy.

• Consumers

They provide direct contact and feedback between customers and producers, so you can be sure how your vegetables are grown and meat produced.

They help to improve diet and nutrition by providing access to fresh food.

continued overleaf >

69

farmers' markets continued >

• Consumers

They play an important role in educating the consumer as to the production and origin of their food.

They can be a source of information and inspiration on how to cook and prepare fresh ingredients.

• The Environment

They help reduce food miles, thus vehicle pollution, noise, and fossil fuel use.

They help to reduce packaging.

They encourage more environmental production practices, such as organic or pesticide free.

They encourage farm diversification and hence bio-diversity.

• The Community & Local Economy

They help bring life into towns and cities aiding regeneration.

They encourage social interaction particularly between rural and urban communities.

They stimulate local economic development by increasing employment, encouraging consumers to support local business, and thus keeping the money within the local community.

They attract business to retailers in the vicinity.

They can encourage the unemployed and under-employed to develop new skills, self confidence and income generating possibilities.

They play an important role in Local Agenda 21 and other Council initiatives established to increase the environmental sustainability of government policies, local communities, and businesses.

What's wrong with supermarkets?

Supermarkets wield immense power over the way food is grown, bought and eaten in our country. Yes, they offer convenience but at what price? Supermarkets provide what the modern consumer allegedly wants, easy access to a wide range of good value food. Millions of tonnes of food are transported around the globe to reach their shelves every day. And through loyalty cards, they know exactly who their shoppers are and what they want, from special offers to all night store opening; larger parking lots and banking facilities, it's hard to resist the lure and easy accessibility of the big multinationals. So why should we? Because they are strangling our food industry, that's why.

75% of food retailing in the UK is controlled by the big four (Tesco, Asda, Sainsbury's and Morrison's). We lost a fifth of local shops and services between 1995 and 2000 and every time a supermarket opens, on average 276 jobs are lost. In contrast the benefits of local shops are that they create employment, less packaging is required as products are more likely to be sold loose and they foster a sense of community spirit and awareness.

How supermarkets reel us in:

It is common for supermarkets to use unethical tactics to lure shoppers. Here are a few that you might recognise:

Use of the word 'local'

Although widely used and celebrated on fresh produce and meat, this label can actually mean 'grown in this country'. And even if it is locally produced, unfortunately due to the centralisation of supermarket distribution, chances are it's been driven halfway round the country for processing and packaging anyway.

Loss Leaders

This means when staples such as bread, milk, tinned tomatoes etc are sold below their market value to entice shoppers. This impacts badly on the farmers, whilst the supermarkets make up profits in other less conspicuous areas such as fresh produce.

Loyalty Cards

This generous gesture from your big friendly supermarket to save money in store actually provides a fabulous opportunity to collect huge amounts of data on each and every one of its shoppers. And data is a valuable commodity. 60% of people in the UK own a loyalty card, 11 million of which are Nectar award cards. These cards do indeed encourage customer loyalty as consumers shop in their chosen store in order to accumulate points. And meanwhile, the happy shopper's profile can be analysed to provide useful information all about their shopping habits. Ever received a supermarket flyer through the door that seems uncannily insightful, focussing on just the little luxuries you like, at discounted prices? Big Brother has his eye on you and your fancies. See **www.nocards.org** for more information.

BOGOF

The Buy One, Get One Free offer encourages us to consume more than we need. How much of this extra food actually gets eaten? To avoid unnecessary waste of food, packaging and money it is better to stick to your normal quantities and try not to get drawn into these false economies.

How to be an Ethical Shopper: food

- **Get creative.** Choose a more pleasant shopping experience by checking out farmers' markets and local shops. Support small local producers for the feel-good factor, absent from supermarket shopping. This also reduces the fossil fuel emissions associated with transporting food. Fresh food is healthier as it has a higher nutritional value and is less likely to have the extra chemicals used to preserve food during storage and transit.

- **Avoid buying exotic or non-seasonal produce,** especially airfreighted food such as mangetout, grapes and mangoes

- **Join a vegetable box scheme**. This is a box containing freshly picked, organic, usually locally grown produce delivered weekly to your door or to a local drop off point. Box scheme operators usually offer small, medium and family size boxes. The vegetables in the box will often vary from week to week depending on the season. The Soil Association (SA) has details of UK veg box schemes online at **www.whyorganic.org** and keen greenies can even find out how to set up a vegetable box scheme if there is not one in the local area using the SA site

- **Set up a Community Supported Agriculture (CSA) scheme.** The principle is that the customer pays in advance for a share of a particular farmer's produce. The farmer draws up his plans for the year and customers sign up to purchase a share of the yield. It brings the customer one step nearer the grower than even farmers' markets do and ensures that the farmers know at the beginning of the planting season that they have a guaranteed market for their produce. The system originated in Japan and is well established in the USA – in the UK it is still in its infancy, but is beginning to grow. For more information see the Soil Association website for pages on CSA and 'Subscription Farming' at **www.soilassociation.org**

- **Wherever possible, walk, cycle or use public transport** to get to the shops or farmers' market

- **Receipt watch.** Check out how much you spend on ethical purchase such as fairtrade and organic goods and work out where the best deals are.

continued... >

73

- **Keep requesting what you want** from local stores. The message will sink in eventually especially if you ask friends and family to do the same

- **Find a food co-op** in your area, making wholefoods much more affordable for everyone. If you can't find one, why not consider setting up your own?

- **Grow some of your own** organic food. If you only have a small garden or no garden try growing herbs and salads, perhaps in a window box

- **A WEN report called 'Sustainable Sustenance'** offers shoppers tips on how to reduce food miles. It compares the journeys different foods make and the CO_2 emissions they cause, and answers the perennial question "which is best, organic, fairly traded, local or seasonal?" You can download the report from their site at **www.wen.org.uk**

- **Eat more fresh food** and enjoy preparing meals from raw ingredients. If unnecessary packaging frustrates you, try leaving it at the check-out! Avoid 'convenience' foods and pre-prepared highly processed and packaged meals

- **Where you can't buy local, choose organic and fairtrade** to ensure that farmers in developing countries are being paid a fair price and do not have to work with harmful chemicals

- **Make your own.** A good place to start is with the daily loaf – it really is simple to make bread and there are lots of inspiring recipes online to get you started

And if you are a bit of an eco activitist, get involved in these actions:

- **Find Fairtrade 'Order Up' cards online at www.fairtrade.org.uk**

- **Find out whether your local store is a member of the Ethical Trading Initiative (ETI) at www.ethicaltrade.org**

- **Lobby local government** to introduce a legally binding code of conduct to ensure that all suppliers in the chain are treated fairly

- **Get hold of a copy of your supermarket's Corporate Social Responsibility Report** and point out areas in which they could improve.

- **When you shop in a supermarket**, send your till receipt to head office with a letter asking how much farmers were paid for your trolley load.

Transport, travel and tourism

Ethical Shopping – Cars

Travel plays a major part in climate chaos – the pollution emitted by cars and planes contributes up to a third of greenhouse gases now and by 2020 transport is predicted to be the UK's biggest contributor.

Half the population flies at least once a year and on average each of us travels around 6,000 miles by car.

84% of cars used for work purposes have only one occupant.

As a nation we under-invest in public transport, such as buses and trains, which could potentially provide a solution to our car-addicted culture. Budget airlines encourage us to jet off around the world, sometimes for under a tenner.

Other issues that arise from our love of travel include local air pollution, blamed for the rise in asthma sufferers, fatalities and injuries, breakdown of communities and the impact on wildlife and rural environment caused by road building.

So how can we make our travel more ethical? Increase our use of public transport, investigate greener fuels, reduce our car use and seriously consider each and every flight we plan to take and evaluate whether it is absolutely necessary.

Does a green car exist?

When looking for a new vehicle it is now possible to choose greener models that run on alternative fuels with cleaner engines. Hybrids, for example, are cars with engines that combine two sources of power; petrol and electricity. The thinking behind this is that it allows for much greater fuel efficiency, about two times more efficient than regular cars. In addition, owners receive benefits in the form of lower road tax, exemption from congestion charges and in some cases grants towards purchase cost. Hybrids include the Toyota Prius, Honda Insight and the Lexus Hybrid Synergy Drive. They look and drive like their conventional counterparts and don't need to be 'plugged in'. The car charges its battery when the brakes are applied, and while the petrol engine is powering the car along at high speeds. When lower speeds are required the engine diverts to the electric battery. They achieve over 60 miles to the gallon and release lower levels of emissions.

Electric cars meanwhile are charged via a mains socket, the greenest vehicles on four wheels, with nearly no emissions. Charge them using electricity from a green supplier and their use creates almost no CO2. The catches are speed, or lack of it, and the fact that they need recharging around every 40 miles, which can be limiting. The GWiz does 40mph, costs around £7000 and according to the manufacturer pays for itself within a year due to no fuel or tax costs. **www.goingreen.co.uk** or **www.evuk.co.uk**

A modern moped can be more energy efficient than a train carrying many passengers. However emissions from a motorbike engine can be more harmful than those from a car. Electric models are now available. Prices start at around £1,500 and they are widely available in the UK. Driving an escooter for 30 miles is equivalent to leaving a light on for a few hours. Zero poisonous emissions created and most even look good. See **www.scootelectric.co.uk**. Also **www.envbike.com**

Alternative Fuels

Hydrogen fuelled vehicles have been manufactured but currently the hydrogen on which they run requires fossil fuels. Scientists are exploring cleaner, greener ways of producing hydrogen through the production of ethanol, an alcohol that is produced when plants ferment. In Brazil, fermented sugar cane fuels many cars. Although ethanol currently costs the same as petroleum it is hoped that this technology will be refined to help replace fossil fuels.

Biofuels produce up to 40% lower emissions. Whilst bio diesel emits CO_2 when burnt, this is mostly balanced out during the growth of the plants that produce it. It is now sold in some garages and as it diverts used oil from chip shops and the restaurant industry it is seen to have duel benefits. See **www.biodiesel.co.uk** for more info. Bio diesel can be used in diesel cars without need for modification **www.vegoilmotoring.com**.

LPG (Liquid Petroleum Gas) is propane, as used in camping stoves – it is a by-product of oil refining and though it is a fossil fuel it has lower greenhouse gas emissions. Most petrol cars can be converted to run off LPG. The conversion costs around £2,000. Once done however, the owner benefits from cheaper fuel and no congestion charge in London.

See www.greenfuel.org.uk or www.lpga.co.uk

How to be an ethical shopper: cars

- **Buy nearly new**. Try not to buy a new car unless you absolutely have to. Be aware however, that newer vehicles pollute less and tend to be more environmentally efficient

- **Buy infrequently** as the second-hand car market is imperfect. It is best to choose a car where you know its history. It is even economic to spend more repairing a vehicle than its market value. Reliability is the key. Once a vehicle becomes unreliable sell it

- **Size is important**. Buy as small as you can for your day to day needs. You may decide you need a big car because you have relatives that live over 400 miles away. If you only visit them twice a year however, and most of your driving is done in a 50-mile radius a big car may be inefficient. By buying a smaller car for the majority of driving and renting a bigger car for the long trips you will save money

- **Consider sharing** a car between the family, or even neighbours, instead of running two or more cars

- **Buy a fuel-economic car**. The fuel economy of similar sized cars using the same type of fuel can vary as much as 45%. The ETA's Car Buyer's Guide gives an accurate assessment of all cars on the market. **www.eta.co.uk**

The most ethical car?

See the Environmental Transport Association's car buyer's guide online at **www.eta.co.uk** to check almost every model available in the UK today, its emissions and efficiency data. Recently Ethical Consumer magazine voted Peugeot, Citroen, Rover, MG and VW at the top of the list for most ethical car manufacturers.

When we consider the eco-credentials of a car we often look for fuel efficiency, engine size and whether it can run on alternative fuels. But this doesn't take into account the fact that quarter of a car's environmental pollution and 20% of its overall energy expenditure occurs during manufacture. To this end, the most ethical choice is usually to opt for a second-hand car.

Other ways of travelling more efficiently in your car:

Consider **planning** as many jobs as possible in one trip. Aim to get as much as you can out of the journey. Five jobs in one trip is better for the environment than five trips!

- **Do not use the car for short journeys**, if your journey is less than half a mile then walk or cycle

- **Avoid congested areas** and so reduce travel time

- **Only travel in the rush hour if you absolutely have to.**

- **Time shift your journey**, a twenty minute delay could make all the difference to time in the car

- **Traffic Sharing** can benefit the environment by lowering emissions and at the same time can allow you more time for other activities. Sharing the school-run, for example, with a roster of parents reduces congestion and fuel usage

There are other ways of making car-ownership greener. Try:

- **Fuel saving tyres** from Firestone, designed to reduce fuel consumption. **www.firestone.eu**. Keep tyres inflated to the correct pressure

- **Natural cleaning wax** for your car body from Zymol. A water-based product without petroleum solvents, this product contains coconut, beeswax, vitamin E and aloe vera to leave your vehicle feeling really pampered! **www.zymol.com**

- **Lift sharing or car pooling** where you share a lift or a car. See **www.liftshare.com** or **www.citycarclub.org** for more info.

Air Travel

Currently air travel is responsible for 5% of carbon emissions but it is the UK's fastest growing cause of global warming. The amount of carbon dioxide emitted by air travel doubled between 1990 and 2004.

Three quarters of air travel is classified as 'leisure', meaning those of us taking to the skies in search of sunnier climes, exotic wild locatons, beautiful beaches and a different culture. But conversely air travel and ill-managed tourism are the very culprits that are destroying the natural beauty and indigenous cultures we are seeking.

Whilst budget flights are sold on the basis that it is a no-frills service, this is far from the case – the low prices are due to fierce competition between the airlines and Government subsidies. Aviation is one of the most heavily subsidised industries with air fuel still exempt from tax. The average UK tax payer supports the aviation industry to the tune of £557 per year.

Harmful gases emitted during air travel are released into a very fragile part of the atmosphere, so the effect of the emissions are actually doubled. We need to minimise air travel and work out alternative ways to travel. We can choose to holiday locally, use other communication methods for business and try to find other methods of travel such as trains.

Profile: Responsible Travel

Justin Francis, co-founder of **www.responsibletravel.com** says: "We all need to fly less, a lot less. One way to do this is to cut out the dramatic increase in short breaks on cheap flights. The only way that this will happen is if the price of flights rises considerably. We need to tell the politicians that we will only vote for parties that are prepared to make the tough choices required to make this happen. We'll all need to holiday closer to home, and travel by train more. Over the next 3 years responsibletravel.com will very significantly increase the number of eco places to stay – enabling you to avoid flying. When we do fly we need to ensure our holiday benefits local communities and reduces other environmental impacts, and we need to offset the emissions."

What is offsetting?

You can pay for trees to be planted to 'offset' the environmental costs of flying. Future Forests at **www.futureforest.com** charges £8.50 per tree and calculates that five trees will cover the CO2 produced during a flight from London to Australia. Offsetting your carbon emissions is certainly better than doing nothing. But **better still would be to avoid creating the emissions in the first place.** Sinkswatch has an issue with us atoning for wasteful behaviour using the increasingly popular 'carbon neutralising' payoff. They say that trees need to reach maturity, which may take ten years or so before they can hope to absorb the level of CO2 caused by air travel for example. Visit **www.sinkswatch.org** for more info.

Other ways of offsetting the emissions?

One of the companies that offers alternative carbon off-setting is Climate Care. The idea is that you pay extra to support lower carbon dioxide initiatives (such as low energy light bulbs or more efficient wood burning stoves in tourism destinations) to compensate for the amount of carbon dioxide that your flight emits.

Although carbon offsetting must not create permission for us to keep on flying to anywhere near the level that we do now, and the calculations required are still being improved, it does serve to neutralise the emissions of flights. If it was made compulsory across the airline industry rather than being an option for tourists it would provide a short term alleviation to the problem.

How to be an ethical shopper: holidays

- **Stay in the UK**. With our many miles of coastline and beautiful countryside the UK can provide just as pleasurable a holiday experience as going abroad

- **Support local businesses** – stay in local hotels, visit local restaurants etc. Choose the independents over the big multinationals

- **Go organic** – find out more about organic places to stay in the UK at **www.organicholidays.com**

- Try an active holiday on a working organic farm. **www.wwoof.org**

- **Use www.seat61.com** to find an alternative method of transport rather than flying

- **Think about who profits from your holiday**. Package holidays are notoriously poor at wealth distribution with 4/5^{ths} going straight to the multi-national travel operators

- **Practise the same ethics that govern your energy and water use at home**. The average tourist uses 10 times the amount of natural resources as a local resident. Re-use your towel and request that laundry is done only once a week

- **Try www.greenglobe21.com** to find out which of the world's airlines, hotels and travel agents meet the environmental standards set by the World Travel and Tourism Council

- **Tip generously** – tourism has a bad reputation for low wages

- Get hold of a copy of **Tourism Concern's *Ethical Travel Guide***. See resources for more information (Travel/Read).

Tourism

Up to 20 million UK residents holiday abroad every year, spending on average £800 a time. Many of these holidays are organised through the big four travel agencies (Thomson, Thomas Cook, Going Places and First Choice) – the rates paid to the locals in the destination country will not be the most generous. Up to four fifths of the money spent on a package holiday ends up in the bank account of the travel agency. Therefore the beneficiary of such holidays is not the local residents, as many tourists believe but a small number of multinational companies. In contrast independent travellers can expect their money to benefit the local economy. When travelling, ethical consumers can have the most positive impact by choosing to support local shops and businesses.

The United Nations World Tourism Organisation states that one in 10 jobs around the world is in tourism, and adds that tourism is growing fastest in developing countries. In 10 of the world's poorest 50 countries tourism is a significant and growing economic factor. Many of these countries lack any real alternative to tourism as their only real assets are their cultures and natural environments.

Ecotourism is a growing industry and describes trips in which the responsible traveller visits natural areas and helps to conserve the local environment, whilst supporting the local people. There are no official guidelines so anyone can use the term eco-tourism to describe what they are offering but a bit of probing usually reveals any 'green wash'.

What is responsible travel?

When we visit beautiful places it's natural to want our holidays to have a positive impact on local people and their environments. Responsible travel is about more authentic holiday experiences that enable you to get a little bit more out of your travels, and give a little bit more back to destinations and local people. All holidays have positive and negative impacts locally. Responsible travel maximises the benefits, and minimises the negative effects of tourism.

Before you book your holiday

• **Plan your route** to minimise carbon emissions – travel by train and public transport where possible, and minimise internal flights. There are some great ideas for train travel almost anywhere in the world on this web site: **www.seat61.com**

• **Minimise flying** time and stopovers – the worst carbon emissions are emitted during take off and landing. For the flights that you cannot avoid, offset the carbon emissions of your flight using a carbon calculator. That way the money is invested in carbon reducing initiatives around the world, offsetting the emissions caused by your flight

• **Ask to see the tour operator's policy for responsible tourism.** Make sure it explains how they minimise environmental impacts and support the local economy.

Before you travel

• **Read** up on local cultures and learn a few words of the local language – travelling with respect earns you respect

• **Remove all excess packaging** – waste disposal is difficult in remote places and developing countries

• **Ask your tour operator for specific tips** for responsible travel in your destination

• **Ask your tour operator/hotel** if there are useful gifts that you could pack for your hosts, local people or schools

• **Ask your tour operator whether there are local conservation or social projects** that you could visit on your trip, and if/how you could help support them.

Green tourism tips:

- **Buy local** produce in preference to imported goods

- **Hire a local guide** – you'll discover more about local culture and lives, and they will earn an income

- **Do not buy** products made from endangered species, hardwoods or ancient artefacts

- **Respect local cultures**, traditions and holy places – if in doubt ask advice or don't visit

- **Use public transport**, hire a bike or walk when convenient – it's a great way to meet local people on their terms and reduce pollution and carbon emissions

- **Use water sparingly** – it's very precious in many countries and tourists tend to use far more than local people

- **Remember** that local people have different ways of thinking and concepts of time, this just makes them different not wrong – cultivate the habit of asking questions (rather than the Western habit of knowing the answers).

Without getting into the intricacies of composting toilets how can the tourist decide between the genuine and the not so genuine? Justin Francis of Responsible Travel offers 10 ways to tell if your hotel is really eco (rather than just 'greenwashing').

1) **Ask the owner** if they have a written policy regarding the environment and local people. If it's not written down ('yeah, yeah we do all that stuff ') then it probably means there are not taking it seriously

2) Ask them to describe the single **contribution to conservation** or local people that they are most proud of

3) Ask them how they **measure their contribution** to conservation and local communities

4) Ask how many **local people they employ**, what % this is of the total, and whether any are in management positions

5) Ask them what they have **specifically done to help protect the environment** and support conservation, and which local charities they work with

6) Ask them **what % of produce and services are sourced locally**/ from within 25km of the hotel

7) Ask them how they treat **waste water** (coral and other wildlife is being destroyed by Caribbean hotels pumping effluent out to sea), and how they heat their building (solar is better than firewood, which can cause deforestation)

8) Ask them what information and advice is provided to tourists on **local cultures and customs**

9) Ask them if they **employ guides from the local community** (local guides not only provide unmatched insights into local cultures, but are also aware of areas/behaviour that might cause offence among local people

10) Ask them for ideas on how you might **get involved with local people** and conservation in a worthwhile and rewarding way for you and the destination.

Household goods

Household Goods

In this chapter we take a look at household appliances and furniture and discover how to choose the most eco-friendly and energy efficient models.

The Cooker

This is the most energy hungry appliance in the home, so it is important that we choose wisely when looking for a new model, both in terms of the environment and our pocket. Fan ovens require less energy than conventional because they reduce the heating up time, so they work out more cost effective and energy efficient. Gas ovens emit less carbon than their electric counterparts, so try to choose gas over electric. A UK study showed that the carbon intensity of cooking with gas was 0.05kgC/k WH compared to 0.12kgC/k Wh. If you do use electric though switch to a green electricity supplier, which will help to cut carbon emissions. Look for the EU Energy rating, found on all cookers and ovens – this grades products on an A to G basis, A is the best.

Fridges and freezers

It is worthwhile taking a look into the ethics of the company behind your white goods. Ethical Consumer magazine's report into fridges and freezers in 2005 found a couple of worrying links. "The Wallenberg family, which controls Electrolux, has fingers in dam building, military and nuclear projects, as does the US company General Electric which part owns Hotpoint, Creda, Bosch and Siemens." This means that in purchasing products from these manufacturers you may be inadvertently supporting activity that you do not agree with, such as nuclear development. Most of the products on sale in the UK are manufactured either here or in Europe which involves less transportation and the environmental costs that involves.

All fridges and freezers need a coolant gas to work. Two ozone-depleting gases once used in fridges, CFCs and HCFCs, have now been phased out in the EU. They were largely replaced by HFCs (hydrofluorocarbons), a gas with the global warming potential of around 3,200 times that of CO_2. Furthermore, the manufacture of HFCs is directly linked to the production of organochlorines, a class of chemicals that are persistent and toxic, and have been targeted for phase out.

Unfortunately, there is no specific phase-out date for HFCs yet. At the Kyoto Summit in 1997, the EU agreed to reduce the emissions of six greenhouse gases, including HFC, by 8% below 1990 levels by 2010.

Before CFCs were developed in the 1930s, hydrocarbon gases – propane, isobutane and cyclopentane – were widely used in refrigeration. They are by far the best choice of gas because they don't damage the ozone layer and don't contribute significantly to global warming, (although they do originate from crude oil). In addition, hydrocarbon fridges have been found to be nearly always more energy efficient than equivalent models using HFCs and CFCs.

Greenpeace has been campaigning against HFCs for a long time and with some success. It pioneered the use of 'greenfreeze' hydrocarbon gases in the early 1990s and now these gases are becoming industry standard in domestic refrigeration in Europe, China, Japan, Latin America and Australia. The first company to use the greenfreeze technology throughout its range was Iceland and now Greenpeace endorses the KYOTO range of fridges and freezers.

Reduce, Reuse and Recycle

UK households discard 2.5 million fridges every year containing an estimated 2,000 tonnes of CFCs and HCFCs. Many will also contain the global warming gas HFC. Since January 2002, all fridges must have their coolant gases and insulation removed before they can be recycled or scrapped to stop these chemicals from being released into the atmosphere. Your local authority still has a responsibility to take your old fridge away. Some do it for free, others charge up to £30 or you could take it to the local domestic refuse site yourself.

How to be an ethical shopper: fridges and freezers

- When you're ready to replace your fridge, it is worth looking for A+ or A++ rated ones, which are the most energy-efficient and cheapest to run

- Insist on a hydrocarbon (R600a) one which might be labelled 'CFC & HFC free'

- Choose the smallest possible model to fulfill your needs

- Freezers consume the most energy of all refrigeration products so try to do without one if possible

- If you need a freezer, chest freezers tend to be more efficient as the cold air doesn't seep out so much when you open the door

- Avoid Frost-Free freezers, as they use on average 45% more energy than manually defrosted models.

How to be an ethical shopper: washing machines

• Choose the smallest washing machine that will fulfil your needs

• Look for the EU Energy rating and choose an energy efficient A rated product

• Look for newer models with an eco button that allows you to reduce the temperature of the wash

• Always fill the machine and wash on a 30° wash where possible

• Switch to a green energy supplier to ensure that the electricity used to run your machine is cleaner and greener.

How to be an ethical shopper: vacuum cleaners

• Try and buy secondhand

• Check out the old style carpet sweepers that are manual and just require a little extra exertion

• If you are purchasing a new model look for the product with the highest suction.

Energy and heating

Boilers

There are more efficient boilers available on the market nowadays so if you are considering replacing your old one look for a gas condensing, or even a solar powered system. They may cost more initially but are cheaper to run and save energy so make more sense in the long run. The difference between the condensing and non condensing boilers is that the former tend to run on about 90% efficiency as opposed to 70%. There are some subsidies available from local authorities who have signed up to the scheme at **www.green-boilers.co.uk**. Shoppers will also find that boilers now carry an energy efficiency label with a grading from A to G, A being the most efficient.

95

Furniture

A recent report stated that the UK is the world's third largest importer of illegal timber. So it is likely that some of us have wooden furniture from illegal logging practices sitting pretty in our homes. Of course this has implications on global warming because deforestation in the Southern Hemisphere is responsible for the second largest amount of greenhouse gas emissions in the world. Greenpeace first brought the subject of illegal logging to the public consciousness over ten years ago. Today some 14.6 million hectares of forest is lost every year, an area larger than England. At least 90% of the forest loss is due to human activities; urban development, illegal logging, forest clearance (for agriculture or plantations), road building and mining. WWF aim to protect, manage and restore the world's most important forests under its global Forests for Life programme. Find out more at **www.wwf.org.uk**.

All the timber and nearly all the paper products used in everyday life come from forests. With this huge demand it is essential that forests are managed sustainably. **Look out for the Forest Stewardship Council (FSC) logo.**

Ethical consumers can access a visual guide to tropical hardwoods at **www.panda.org**. When you purchase tropical hardwoods, spruce and even pine it is likely that you are contributing to forest destruction in the developing world and in Eastern Europe.

So what are the alternatives?

Arbor Vetum produce a beautiful range of furniture made from reclaimed teak. All items are certified by **FSC. www.arborvetum.co.uk**

Reel furniture provides an ethical approach to their furniture range. Using green materials for their furniture has raised awareness of ethical issues involving timber imports and its effect on our environment. See their products at: **www.reelfurniture.co.uk**

Quirky pieces such as the recycled cardboard sofa and twig bench made by the **Wildlife Trusts in Gloucestershire** available from **www.nigelsecostore.com**

Solid wood **bedroom furniture** made from sustainable sources. **www.alphabeds.co.uk**

One of the **major retailers** who have committed to the **FSC** sourcing accreditation is **B&Q**. Find your nearest store at **www.diy.com**

Beautiful **one off pieces of furniture** made from reclaimed materials at **www.desirabledebris.co.uk**

Rom Tam Design specialises in low impact furniture. Find out more at **www.eco-furniture.co.uk**

Fancy reclining in a pink shopping trolley? At **www.ecohomestore.co.uk** you'll find one of these and more unusual designs to spice up your front room

Gorgeous goods available from **Ethnic Style** at **www.ethnicstyle.com**

Handmade bespoke upholstered furniture is available from **Harland's Organic Furnishings** see **www.organic-furnishings.co.uk**

Beautiful handcrafted chairs can be purchased from **www.malcolmdavidsmith.co.uk**

Organic Furniture www.organicfurniture.co.uk makes unique designs from reclaimed Sussex oak

David Colwell is an award winning furniture designer. His work can be found at **www.davidcolwell.com**.

Cleaning products

Six-thousand infant and toddler accidents each year are attributed to chemical cleaning products.

Could housework be doing you harm? According to the Environmental Protection Agency in the US, levels of pollutants in the home can be up to 100 times higher than those outdoors. Studies have also found that children exposed to high levels of certain chemicals found in cleaning products are more likely to have asthma. This is not surprising when you learn of the array of chemicals contained within many household cleaners.

Over the last fifty years, cleaning product manufacturers have upped the anti in the war against dirt in our homes. We are now faced with an entire aisle in the supermarkets packed with products that promise to make our whites whiter and our toilet bowls sparkle. But we don't need to wage chemical war on household dirt and dust. In fact a little dirt is good for us, encouraging the development of a healthy immune system. However, that argument might not cut it when your mother-in-law comes to stay so let's look at the alternatives to chemical cleaners.

What are the alternatives?

There are a number of 'natural' brands available now on the green cleaning scheme.

There are the bigger brands such as Ecover, Earth Friendly Products and Bio D, available in health food stores and supermarkets. And in recent years some smaller companies have sprung up, most notably Nest, Home Scents and Natural Cleaning. Choosing alternatives such as these ensures that you are not contributing to the problem of chemicals leaching into the water system every time you wash the dishes or do a load of laundry.

What to avoid

Many big brands rely on petroleum-based surfactants in cleaning products to remove dirt and grease. These petroleum derivatives such as sodium lauryl sulphate are slow to biodegrade and during the degradation process may form compounds that are more hazardous than the original substance.

Currently it is not possible to identify the ingredients in most cleaning products as there is no law stipulating that they should be listed on the packaging. The labels that state the product is biodegradable are misleading as all such products will biodegrade sooner or later, it's the time that it takes to do so and the chemicals released in the process that we need to worry about.

Unfortunately animal testing is common for the major ingredients within conventional cleaning products. Look for the BUAV symbol to be sure that your cleaning products haven't been tested on animals.

A whiter shade of pale

Bleach is a hazardous substance that affects our wildlife in rivers and seas and also has a potentially dangerous effect on humans. When chlorine based bleaches react with ammonia they release chlorine gas. Ecover and Bio D have choosen not to produce a bleach product because of its environmental impact. Their toilet cleaners contain acid instead which dislodges waste rather than sterilises it.

Packaging

The main ingredient of most cleaning products is water; when this is packaged and transported round the country to shops and supermarkets this wastes a great deal of unnecessary energy. Concentrated products are a better choice. Look out for the recycling symbol on the bottle to check that it can be recycled. Some local health food shops offer a refilling service for green cleaning products. And if yours doesn't yet, why not ask?

Of course, you can avoid excess packaging altogether by choosing household alternatives such as lemon, vinegar and bicarbonate of soda.

Profile: Natural House

A recent study showed that more than 80% of consumers would choose an organic alternative for cleaning their home if it were widely available. In answer to this the Soil Association has just certified the first range of organic cleaners. Free from the harsh chemicals and irritants found in many household products, the **Natural House range** comprises five products. The products including Window Spa and Surface Spa are simply formulated, based on recipes from our grandparent's generation. They are made using traditional ingredients such as vinegar and plant essences combined with new ingredients such as the Quillaja plant, sourced from South America where it is renowned for its gentle detergent properties. Although this does involve some 'cleaning' miles, ethical living has to be about balance. For fragrance, the range uses organic essential oils rather than synthetic perfumes. Find out more at **www.natural-house.co.uk**

Entertainment

Television and DVDs

Approx 2.5 million TV sets are thrown away every year in this country. Ending up in landfill these leach toxic substances and when consumers purchase new sets, account for a huge waste of resources. Most televisions are made from 50% glass and also contain brominated flame retardants (BFRs), which can have a serious effect on health. See **www.foe.co.uk** for information on the Friends of the Earth campaign to ban BFRs; or, go to **www.impactpublishing.co.uk** for their book *The Toxic Consumer*. Liquid crystal display models are easier to recycle than conventional televisions but also use a large number of raw materials and energy in their production.

If equipment is still in working order it can be freecycled **www.freecycle.org** or taken to the local charity shop. Some civic amenity tips will recycle old television sets for scrap and reusable parts.

Energy

The energy used to power our TV sets creates 7 million tonnes of CO2 every year. Of course, if we all switched them off at the wall, rather than relying on the stand-by function we could shave a huge chunk off this figure and according to Friends of the Earth save £12 million in electricity bills countrywide. Luckily manufacturers are taking this energy consumption into account when designing new models and television sets and other electrical equipment are gradually becoming more energy efficient.

In addition to the energy and raw materials used in manufacture, the energy wasted whilst in use and the destruction caused when dumped in favour of a new model, the television can also affect our health. They emit electro-magnetic radiation, which has been linked to headaches, migraine and depression. Avoid sitting too close, watching for prolonged periods or siting equipment in bedrooms, especially children's rooms. It is possible to buy EMF harmonising equipment for television, computers and mobile phones but as I have not tested the efficacy of these products myself, cannot recommend them. Find out more at **www.sulis-health.co.uk**

How to be an ethical shopper: TV

- Look for secondhand equipment such as television, video or DVD player where possible. Try local free ad papers or freecycling network

- When your TV breaks, see if it can be repaired before replacing it. If not, make sure it is recycled

- Choose smaller models that require less energy in manufacture and when in use

- Check out the bamboo LCD TV available from **www.buyorganics.co.uk**. It's about as attractive as a television is going to get made from natural bamboo!

- Share a TV with your neighbours. Controversial yes, but you get to shave money off household bills through saving electricity and TV license costs and you might end up fitter too with less time spent in front of the box.

Profile: Green TV

Green TV is a broadband TV station dedicated to providing a platform for environmental films. Launched in partnership with the United Nations Environment Programme and Greenpeace the site has over 150 films available to view on demand from a diverse range of organisations, tackling issues ranging from climate change to ecotechnologies. Worth a visit for Grocery Store Wars in which an all edible cast including Cuke Skywalker, Obi Wan Cannoli, and Chewbrocolli fight DarthTata and The Dark Side of the Farm for control of the supermarket. **www.green.tv**

Films to watch:

The Corporation explores the nature and spectacular rise of the dominant institution of our time. Footage from pop culture, advertising, TV news, and corporate propaganda, illuminates the corporation's grip on our lives.

Supersize Me – Morgan Spurlock set out to interview experts in 20 US cities, including Houston – the "Fattest City" in America – whilst at the same time conducting his own personal experiment – to eat nothing but McDonalds for 30 days straight. Gross but fascinating.

Coffee, Take it Fairly – Three women who are fairtrade coffee producers from the community of Los Alpes, northern Nicaragua, describe with great pride their families, their farms and the difference that fairtrade has made to their lives. Produced by Anita Sandhu & Nicaragua Solidarity Campaign 2006.

An Inconvenient Truth – The block buster best selling film by ex-Vice President of the United States, Al Gore, this is a powerful battle cry about the action necessary to stop global warming.

Books

Greenpeace, with their campaign against deforestation of ancient forests, are making progress in transforming the book industry. To date, Pearson and Random House, two of the biggest publishers in the UK are committed to ensuring that the paper they use is ancient forest friendly – either from recycled waste or from FSC certified sources. Books now being printed on FSC/recycled paper include the latest Harry Potter and Michael Morpurgo's Kensuke's Kingdom. Read more at **www.greenpeace.org.uk**.

Avid readers can log on to **www.readitswapit.co.uk** and swap titles after they have read them. Another site, **www.greenmetropolis.com** offers readers the chance to sell their books on, making money and saving the planet at the same time, as a percentage of every sale is donated to The Woodland Trust. Ron Hornbaker creator of **www.bookcrossing.com** decided to give secondhand books the mystery they deserve. Once you have finished a book, log it onto the site and then loose it into the wild by leaving it on a train or on a bench to be picked up by a stranger. You can then hopefully track the book and the pleasure it has given others through the site.

Computers

Computers have now become an essential part of our lives. As new technologies are developed, we often choose to replace our older systems with the latest available products. Inevitably, this will have a negative impact upon the environment and affect computer supply chains world-wide. These are issues which are easy to forget each time we turn our computers on, as the polluting materials and hours of labour needed to produce each machine are hidden from view. Considering this, does an ethical computer exist?

Firstly, let's take a look at what's inside the average computer.

Despite the recent implementation of European Union (EU) regulations to restrict the use of certain toxics in electronic equipment, hazardous substances and processes still form a part of the production process. Some of the toxic substances still in use include:

Brominated Flame Retardants (BFRs): used in printed circuit boards, cables, wires and plastic for computer casings. They can affect learning and memory functions in humans.

Cadmium: used in rechargeable batteries and computer screens. Can affect the nervous system.

Mercury: used in batteries, may be harmful to the nervous system and toxic in high doses.

Lead: used in cathode ray tubes, can be harmful to the nervous system and poisonous in high doses.

Flux: its chemical reaction facilitates the soldering process. In high concentrations it can cause dizziness, unconsciousness and even death. High levels can also cause depression in the central nervous system.

With most big brand companies outsourcing the production of various computer components to multiple suppliers, health and safety standards within these supply chains have become the focus of environmental and workers' rights groups. For example, Greenpeace International's 'Eliminate toxic chemicals' campaign has produced a Green Electronics Guide which includes a rating of computer companies based on their use of hazardous materials (see table below). It also scores companies on their product take-back.

Greenpeace's PC manufacturer ratings

Company name	Grade	Score out of 10 in which high is good
Dell	Points lost for not yet having models without the worst chemicals. Strong support for take back.	7
Samsung	Points for toxic phase out but not good on take back and recycling.	5
Sony	Some models without the worst chemicals, but bad on precautionary principle and take back	4.7
Hewlett Packard	Timelines only for toxics phase out plan. Good on amounts recycled	4.7

Toshiba	Timelines only for toxics phase out plan. Good on amounts recycled.	**3**
Fujitsu-Siemens	Points for some models free of worst chemicals, but poor on take back.	**3**
Apple	Low scores on almost all criteria	**2.7**
Acer	Should do better on all criteria	**2.3**
Lenovo	The lowest score of all companies	**1.3**

This is adapted from the Greenpeace Green Electronics Guide. It scores PC manufacturers out of 10 on their global policies and practice on eliminating harmful chemicals and on taking responsibility for their products once they are discarded by consumers. Companies are ranked solely on information that is publicly available. See Greenpeace website for more information about the companies profiled: **www.greenpeace.org/international/campaigns/toxics**

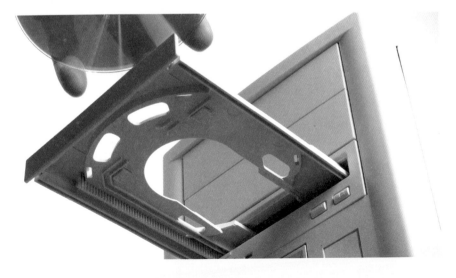

How to be an ethical shopper: computers

• Consider whether you really need a new one – can the old one be upgraded?

• If you have to buy new, make sure that you buy the highest quality possible that can be upgraded in the future, eliminating need for replacement

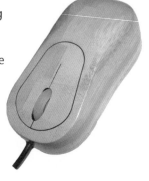

• Ethical Consumer rated the following three companies as the top ethical buys in a recent report. Aries (08716 661616), Evesham (01386 769 600), MESH (08700 468330) and Viglen (01727 201800) scored best on the table for both laptops and desktop computers

• Look for the EU Energy Star label, which shows how energy efficient a product is.

Playtime

Parents spend around £8 billion a year on toys in this country. This figure is echoed in the fact that children have owned on average £11,000 worth of toys by the time they reach adulthood. Many children's toys are made from brightly coloured plastic, a petroleum based product, liable to breakages with built in obsolescence. Often these plastic goods are linked to TV and film characters and therefore have a fashion element built in which encourages their owners to discard them when they move onto the next trend. And with marketing men desperate to sell us this plastic tat for our kids, you can be sure there will be a big new thing just round the corner.

Human rights issues also come into question with the fact that the majority of toys are still produced in factories in China. Some working conditions leave a great deal to be desired. The work is often seasonal and peak production hours such as before Christmas mean that workers are often forced to work long hours in cramped conditions. In September 2005, a report detailing conditions in eleven randomly chosen factories in China producing toys for companies including Mattel and Hasbro found that despite the adoption of company codes of conduct, the abuse of toy workers' rights were still occurring. Violations found included work schedules of more than eighty hours per week, pay rates as low as 59% of the local minimum wage and overcrowded dormitories. Of the eleven sites looked at, only one was abiding by Chinese laws on work time and pay regulations.

End of shelf-life:

Plastic toys cause problems when they are disposed of as incineration releases more noxious chemicals and further contaminates the environment. Plastics and PVC are also difficult to recycle, meaning that much of it ends up in landfills, and here, chemicals can leach out into the soil over time.

An ethical consumer will want to look for those toys made by companies adhering to fairtrade practices, using sustainability sourced wood.

Try the following companies:

• Ptolemy Toys can be found at **www.ptolemytoys.co.uk** offering toys which are made in Europe under fair trade conditions.

• Toys to You. A good selection of fairtrade toys including wooden puzzles and playscenes. **www.toys-to-you.co.uk**

• Globalkids offer a wide range of fairtrade and organic toys because it opens up markets and means they are able to offer many interesting, unusual and hand crafted items that would not reach the general public otherwise. **www.globalkids.co.uk**

• Unusual, ethical toys available online from By Nature at **www.bynature.co.uk**. Great nature kits, recycled cardboard playhouses and solar powered toys.

• The eco-friendly wooden toys at Makes a Change are all Fair Trade and most are made from Rubberwood. This is wood from the same tree that produces natural rubber, and when the tree no longer produces rubber its wood can be made into eco friendly toys. The organic cotton and wool comforters, dolls and rattles are all made from natural, undyed, unbleached and uncoloured organic cotton. Find out more at **www.makesachange.co.uk**

• Great selection of colourful wooden and cotton toys from Green Baby available at **www.greenbabyco.uk**

• Ethical, organic and fair trade toys including organic teddies for birth to two year olds available at Leave Only Footprints **www.lofootprints.co.uk** Rubberwood Peek-a-boo ball £4.99

www.ptolemytoys.co.uk

- Organic hand puppets and recycled cardboard play equipment at **www.love-eco.co.uk**

- Eco-drawing equipment including slate boards and chalk, recycled juice carton pencil cases and much more at The Natural Store **www.thenaturalstore.co.uk**

- Fairtrade instruments at The Green Fairy Godmother **www.greenfairygodmother.co.uk**

- Fairtrade sports equipment including balls, gloves etc. **www.racadillo.com**

- Families of Fairtrade dolls available from **www.naturalnursery.co.uk**

- Jigsaw puzzles and other goodies available at Ecotopia **www.ecotopia.co.uk**

- Wide selection of toys including treehouses and natural paints available at Lessons in Play **www.lessonsinplay.co.uk**

- Beautiful hand-knitted and fairtrade soft toys from Nice Toy Shop **www.nicetoyshop.co.uk**

- Ethically produced toys with a green conscience from **www.toykind.co.uk**

Profile: Globalkids

Rachel Lea-Wilson set up **Globalkids**, an online natural toys shop with her husband Tom last year. She says; "I really wanted to combine my love of children and the environment with my passion for customer service. The thought of achieving a better work life balance in the process, was also a big incentive!" Rachel and Tom have a daughter Mabel who is two, a real whirlwind on legs! Although they work incredibly hard to make Globalkids the successful business it is Rachel says, "we also work hard to make time for family and friends and on a good week I get an hour or two just for me!" **www.globalkids.co.uk**

Profile: Pocomundo

Pocomundo is owned and run by Fiona Keoshgerian and Abi Gurney. This magical toyshop was born over lunch one Sunday when the conversation turned to the lack of quality, environmentally friendly toys available locally. Fiona says, "All wooden toys use wood from sustainable forests and many toys are sourced from Fair Trade suppliers. It is important to us to reduce as well as reuse and recycle everything we can and instead of plastic we have lovely paper bags." Shopping at The Global Village, East Sussex where Pocomundo is based, is certainly a pleasurable experience for parents with its outdoor play area, changing facilities and coffee shop together with a selection of other shops to browse around. On the work/life balance, Fiona explains, "Right from day one we both said that our children would always be our first priority, so work fits around them rather than the other way around. Our children love having mummies who own a toyshop. They like to come in and help, frequently offering their invaluable advice on what's good and not so good!"

www.pocomundo.co.uk

How to be an ethical shopper: toys

- Find a local toy library through your council or organise swaps with friends

- Avoid toys made from plastic

- Encourage imaginative and creative play – dressing up, role and creative play doesn't always require specific toys

- Choose wooden toys with non-toxic, water-based paints and natural finishes such as linseed

- If buying wooden toys, check that they're from FSC certified sources or an equivalent guarantor of managed forests. Look for the FSC logo

- Avoid toys using excess packaging

- Construction toys made from metal are a good choice and also beneficial to your child's development

- Encourage your children to adopt repair, reuse and recycle principles

- Buy toys manufactured in Europe or under Fairtrade Principles

- Donate old toys to toy libraries, charities, playschemes or hospitals rather than throwing them away

- Buy second-hand toys from charity shops and jumble sales

- Avoid 'unnecessary' technology wherever you can.

Money

It makes the world go round doesn't it? And if you don't want your spare cash to bank roll those companies involved in dubious activities, then you had better choose an ethical bank. Banking with an ethical provider means your money will not be used to fund arms dealers, oppressive regimes or deforestation.

What is the history of ethical banking?

Dating back to the nineteenth century, the roots of ethical investment can be found among religious movements including the Quakers and Methodists, whose concerns included issues such as temperance and fair employment conditions. At the beginning of the 1900s, the Methodist Church began investing in the stockmarket, consciously avoiding companies involved in alcohol and gambling. During the twentieth century more churches, charities and individuals began to take account of ethical criteria when making investment decisions.

Initially the US was more advanced in developing the ideology and in 1971 the Pax World Fund was set up which avoided investments associated with the Vietnam War. And then in the 1980s the apartheid regime in South Africa accelerated the promotion of ethical investment.

In 1983 Ethical Investment Research Services (EIRIS) was established as the UK's first independent research service for ethical investors. And then a year later the UK's first ethically screened unit trust was launched by Friends Provident – the Stewardship Fund. Over the last 20 years the growth in ethical investment has been immense.

This growth has also been reflected globally, for example Asia has seen the launch of several ethical funds in places like Japan and Singapore. In Europe there were around 170 ethical funds in 1999, 2 years later the number had grown to over 280 and continues to grow. Over the same period it was estimated that the value of assets involved in some form of socially responsible investment in the US had risen by more than a third to over 2 trillion dollars.

A major boost to the field came in 2000 when it became UK law for occupational pension schemes to say whether they took account of any social, environmental or ethical factors when deciding what stocks to invest in. Since then several other countries have followed suit such as Australia, Sweden and Germany. Pension funds are by far the largest group of shareholders and so have considerable influence over companies – they could be a major vehicle for driving improvements in corporate behaviour.

What's available?

At one end of the spectrum, negative screening looks at unacceptable practices considered to be harmful to people, the environment and animals and excludes any company found to be involved in these undesirable practices.

"Caused based" investments is practised by Triodos Bank (**www.triodos.co.uk**) and this method involves investing in projects that have social and environmental worth.

At the other end of the scale, light green investment policies rule out a few 'dodgy' industries such as arms manufacture. Positive screening describes this method where any company can qualify for a loan as long as they fulfil certain criteria such as sound environmental reporting. Hopefully positive screening is used alongside an Engagement Strategy with investors encouraged to improve the environmental and social policies of the company by agreeing to invest only if certain criteria are met, though this is not necessarily the case.

What is FTSE4Good?

This is the share index for socially responsible investors. Excluding tobacco, nuclear and arms industries, the index benchmarks companies based on their corporate social responsibility (CSR) practices. Investors can use them to identify companies with positive CSR records

Want more information?

An ethical investment report can be downloaded from **www.eiris.org**, home of the Ethical Investment Research Services. Readers will also find lots of information here and the ability to search for an independent financial adviser with expertise in ethical matters.

High street banks

The majority of us hold our main account with one of the four leading banks in the UK. But they don't have such a good track record when it comes to ethics.

The big four; Lloyds, Barclays, HSBC and Natwest have been criticised for their involvement and investment in companies that manufacture arms and contribute to deforestation. None have a serious ethical investment code, yet, and do not produce dedicated social or environmental reports. With high over-drafts and account charges coupled with some top dog salaries of over £10m a year, banks have also been accused of ripping off their customers.

So what are the alternatives?

Ethical banking

Triodos Bank – set up in the Netherlands in 1980, it also has branches in the UK and Belgium. Personal and business savers are offered a range of services similar to most banks, but its business loans are only to organisations involved in sustainable development projects – for example solar and wind energy, organic agriculture, and projects in the developing world. Tel: 0500 008 720, **www.triodos.com**

Ecology Building Society – set up in 1981, is dedicated to improving the environment by promoting sustainable housing and sustainable communities. It uses the money deposited by savers to provide mortgages to those whose plans will be of benefit to the environment. The Ecology provides mortgages for energy efficient housing, ecological renovation, derelict and dilapidated properties and small-scale and ecological enterprise. Tel: 0845 674 5566, **www.ecology.co.uk**

Co-operative Bank – began in 1872 as the savings and loans arm of the Co-operative Wholesale Society. In 1991 its research found that 84% of customers wanted the bank to have a clear ethical policy, which it duly introduced. It will not lend to any companies involved in the arms trade, or whose conduct violates human rights. It supports enterprises with positive social and ethical intentions. Tel: 0845 7212 212, **www.co-operativebank.co.uk**. See also the online bank at **www.smile.co.uk**

Charity Bank – in 2002 Gordon Brown launched the Charity Bank, the UK's first registered charity which is also a bank, regulated like other financial service providers by the Financial Services Authority. The Charity Bank's sole business is to accept deposits in order to make affordable loans for charitable purposes. Individuals can open up a savings account and know that the money they invest is earning social as well as financial returns. Tel: 01732 520029 **www.charitybank.org**

Ethical money Q and A

Q. I have a sum of money that I would like to invest ethically – how can I do it?

A. You are strongly recommended to seek independent financial advice. There are a number of ethical/socially responsible funds that are available to the UK investor. They will all have different ethical investment policies and different ways of applying those policies. A financial adviser with expertise in this field should be able to explain what the differences are between the funds and identify those that would most closely match your ethical priorities. If you want to invest directly in the stockmarket the EIRIS can offer a service that provides an acceptable list of companies based on your own social, environmental and ethical preferences, as well as analysis of existing portfolios. Visit **www.eiris.org** for further information. Also check out **www.ethicalinvestment.org.uk** for a list of ethical financial advisers.

Q. I want to know how ethical my bank/building society is – can you help?

A. EIRIS has a downloadable guide to Responsible Banking on their website. If you are concerned about your bank's practices perhaps you would like to consider banking with one of the banks mentioned in the previous pages?

Q. I am looking for an ethical mortgage – where should I go?

A. You will want to consider if it is the provider of your mortgage, the mortgage product itself or both that you want ethical properties to apply to. Financial circumstances will also need to be taken into account to ensure the mortgage you choose is the right one for you and your situation. Seeking independent financial advice is recommended. Also try **www.ecology.co.uk**

Q. I'm thinking of changing my pension to one that's ethical – can you suggest one?

A. You are strongly recommended to seek independent financial advice. If you have an occupational pension scheme since 2000 these schemes have had to disclose whether any social, environmental or ethical factors are taken into account within the fund's investment selection process. So you will be able to find out if it has a socially responsible investment (SRI) policy and if so what it entails. As a member you can also lobby the scheme's trustees to implement an SRI policy or develop an existing one. With personal pensions, there are a number of ethical funds that can be used as pensions saving vehicles, as well as a number of ethical stakeholder pensions. See **www.uksif.org**, home of the UK Social Investment Forum where visitors can access a quarterly newsletter on socially responsible pension funds.

Q. I am looking for an ethical investment fund – can you recommend one?

A. The EIRIS ethical fund selector has details on the social, environmental and other ethical policies of the ethical funds open to UK investors. See **www.eiris.org**. Try also **www.triodos.co.uk**.

Seven tips for the ethical investor

- Establish which issues are important to you when investing (eg. companies with no involvement in GM or animal testing)

- Decide how much risk you want to take. Shares are more risky than leaving money in a bank account, but the rewards are potentially much higher

- Contact an ethical independent financial adviser (IFA). Find an ethical IFA by looking at the up-to-date information provided by the Ethical Investment Association, the Ethical Investment Research Service, and the UK Social Investment Forum

- There are many ways to green your money. Your adviser may suggest you change your bank account, set up an ISA or start a pension fund. You may want to look at a green mortgage or moving your house contents insurance policy to an ethical provider

- Become a member of a credit union or join a time bank or local trading scheme such as LETS

- Do an annual audit – make sure your money is doing what you want by regularly checking on the interest rates of your bank accounts, the status of your mortgage loan and the ethical performance of the companies you are doing business with

- Make a will. Make sure your money goes to the right people and places.

Profile: Grameen Bank

Grameen Bank (GB), meaning village bank, has reversed conventional banking practice by removing the need for collateral and created a banking system based on mutual trust, accountability, participation and creativity. GB provides credit to the poorest of the poor in rural Bangladesh, a practice known as microcredit. At GB, credit is a cost effective weapon to fight poverty and it serves as a catalyst in the overall development of socio-economic conditions of the poor who have been kept outside the banking orbit on the grounds that they are poor and hence not bankable. Professor Muhammad Yunus, the founder of "Grameen Bank" and its Managing Director, reasoned that if financial resources can be made available to the poor on terms and conditions that are appropriate and reasonable, "these millions of small people with their millions of small pursuits can add up to create the biggest development wonder."

As of January 2007, it has 6.95 million borrowers, 97 percent of whom are women. With 2343 branches, GB provides services in 75,359 villages, covering more than 90 percent of the total villages in Bangladesh. Grameen has contributed to poverty eradication by providing poor women access to loans to raise animals, weave baskets, and engage in other activities making them better able to provide for their families.

Mortgages

Over the course of your mortgage you'll probably be handing over hundreds of thousands of pounds to your mortgage lender. So if the ethical stance of your chosen provider isn't up to scratch, it's time to look at the alternatives.

A mutual building society is probably the best mainstream option for ethical consumers as your money is unlikely to fund any unscrupulous activity. A mutual building society is only involved in mortgages and therefore your money will solely be used to invest in someone else's home purchase.

The **Co-op** offer a carbon neutral mortgage and promise to offset all the CO_2 arising from the household gas and electricity consumption.

Ecology Building Society is a small mutual that funds energy efficient housing projects and eco-friendly development.

Norwich and Peterborough Building Society. Another mutual which promises to plant eight trees a year for five years, enough to absorb the CO_2 produced by the average household.

3

Alternatives

"There is enough on earth for everybody's need, but not for everyone's greed." Mahatma Gandhi

We are draining the world of its finite resources with our ever increasing need to consume. So if we decide to step off and re-evaluate, what can we do to slow down the tide of consumer culture? Let's take a three tiered approach; trading without using money, shopping less and finally not shopping at all. Bit radical this last one, but it's just for a day – unless you get a taste for it.

Trading without money: LETS schemes

LETS Local Exchange Trading Systems or Schemes – are local community-based mutual aid networks in which people exchange all kinds of goods and services with one another, without the need for money. In a LETSystem of several hundred members the range of services offered is extensive. This system creates money but not for the sake of creating money; credits are earned through activity and healthy productivity.

It is hoped that the schemes will revitalise communities throughout Britain. As grassroots initiatives they are open to everyone – people of all ages, skills and abilities; local clubs and associations; voluntary groups, charities, community initiatives; housing co-operatives, small businesses and local services – helping everyone to give and take, connect to new resources, and find a genuine community identity.

LETS offer equal opportunities to all, using a system of community credits, so that direct exchanges do not have to be made. People earn credits by providing a service, and can then spend the credits on whatever is offered by others on the scheme: for example childcare, transport, food, home repairs or the hire of tools and equipment.

Research in about 1996 indicated that at least 40,000 people were involved in some 450 schemes. For more information about LETS groups in your area: **www.letslinkuk.net**

Shop Less

Share things that obviously have a high resource impact, such as cars, lawn-mowers, deep freezers, etc. You might want to ask if you could survive without a fridge. Before the 1950s people used to shop locally and regularly for perishables, and the pantry would keep most things fresh for an acceptable length of time. Another example of buying less would be the radical extension of home and allotment growing, as happened during the second world war. By buying less we do not automatically make a better society, merely a less polluted one. There is still the need to design and implement better ways of running a post-consumer economy. Buy goods which have little or no packaging or make your point by presenting the excess to the manager of the shop. Try to buy more durable goods. Avoid advertised products and the feeling of being manipulated.

Buy Nothing Day

Every year at the end of November, people get together to celebrate Buy Nothing Day, an event that challenges us to switch off from shopping and tune into life. Anyone can take part provided they spend a day without spending. Buy Nothing Day helps to expose the environmental and ethical consequences of consumerism. The developed countries – only 20% of the world population are consuming over 80% of the earth's natural resources, causing a disproportionate level of environmental damage and unfair distribution of wealth.

As consumers we need to question the products we buy and challenge the companies who produce them. What are the true risks to the environment and developing countries? The argument is infinite – while it continues we should be looking for simple solutions – Buy Nothing Day is a good place to start. Of course, Buy Nothing Day isn't about changing your lifestyle for just one day It's important that people make a commitment to consume less, recycle more and challenge companies to clean up and be fair. The supermarket or shopping mall might offer great choice, but this shouldn't be at the cost of the environment or developing countries.

A wide range of activities take place all over the world in celebration of BND including swap parties, free concerts and shows. Hapless shoppers might find that credit card cut-up tables or 'no-shop' zones decked out with carpets and chairs have taken over their city centre shopping malls.

So where did BND come from? Buy Nothing Day started in 1993 by the founders of Adbusters **www.adbusters.org** and is now an international event celebrated in over 55 countries.

And what's the point of it? The idea is to make people stop and think about what and how much they buy and how that affects the environment and developing countries. It's actually quite challenging to last 24 hours without spending any money these days. Hopefully participants feel detoxed from shopping and realise how much it uses up valuable free time.

What is so bad about shopping? It's not shopping in itself that's so harmful, it's what we buy. The two areas that we need to concentrate on are the environment and poverty. We need to consider the way our goods are produced. Increasingly large companies use labour in developing countries to produce goods because it's cheap and there aren't the systems to protect workers like there are in the west.

What about the environment? The raw materials and production methods that are used to make so many of our goods have harmful side affects such as toxic waste, destruction of wild life, and wasted energy. The transport of goods internationally also contributes to pollution especially when many can be produced nationally.

Is one day really going to make a difference? Buy Nothing Day isn't about changing your lifestyle for just one day – it's a lasting relationship – maybe a life changing experience! The aim is to make Buy Nothing Day stick in people's minds so they think about the future and turn their back on the throw-away society we have become.

What can I do? Literally, doing nothing is doing something! And if you feel really motivated you could organise an event to support Buy Nothing Day. A Buy Nothing Day event can be anything from staying at home with a good book to organising a free concert. If this is your first time its best to set your sights on something easy. Ask friends to help and remember groups spring up just for BND.

Here are some tips to help your event run smoothly.

Your event should be fun and engaging. Humour works in a big way – the sillier the better. The public generally love the idea of Buy Nothing Day and many of the events tried over previous years have been well received – below are some ideas.

SHOPPER FREE ZONE Mark out a public area and fill it with people playing games, listening to music and chilling out on sofas or chairs. Hand out balloons with Buy Nothing Day written on them to the bemused onlookers.

CONSUMER MONSTER! Join the Consumer Monster Challenge – take to the streets with a video camera and your own consumer monster activist puppet to spread consumer awareness. Learn how to make your own puppet at **www.consumermonster.com** – Get stitching!

SWAP SHOP Fairly simple idea. Set up a table and ask people to do swaps. Just for fun – leave a set of bogus Porsche keys and see if anyone notices?

Planning your event is key to its success. Hold a few meetings with friends before the day. Ask friends to take on responsibilities, i.e. making posters leaflets and banners – costumes (if needed) and get someone to deal with the publicity and press etc. Let the press and local radio know what you are doing. See **www.buynothingday.co.uk** for more ideas and to find out what others are doing around the world in support of Buy Nothing Day.

Take this one step further and you have **Buy Nothing Christmas www.buynothingchristmas.org**. Here are some ideas for alternative presents:

- A **hand made recipe book** is a good idea, a compilation of recipes from your family and friends. Start collecting them in the summer, edit them and add your own comments.

- **Books on tape** – this is great if you have elderly relatives who find it difficult to read books any longer.

- Try **www.oxfamunwrapped.com**. It allows you to send a gift to developing countries and depending on your budget you can buy chickens, blankets, radios, right up to a travelling theatre!

- **Try doing something;** reading a book, giving a massage, singing a song, writing a poem – for a person.

4

Resources

Clothes:

Clean Clothes campaign – a US site based on encouraging transparency and improving working conditions in the global clothing industry. **www.cleanclothes.org**

Labour Behind the Label www.labourbehindthelabel.org, a campaign that supports garment workers' efforts worldwide to improve their working conditions.

www.cleanupfashion.co.uk for Clean up Fashion site where you can find in depth info on high street retailers.

www.bafts.org.uk – Find fair trade shops in your area on the British Association of Fair Trade Shops website.

Oxfam – NGO involved in education and campaigning. **www.oxfam.org.uk**

www.nosweat.org.uk – campaigning for sweatshop free trade.

www.pan-uk.org – The Pesticide Action Network is working to eliminate the dangers of toxic pesticides, our exposure to them, and their presence in the environment where we live and work.

Home to **People for the Ethical Treatment of Animals** where visitors can find more info about the fur trade and leather industry. **www.peta.org**

Ethical Clothing Retailers:

www.adili.com	www.bishopstontrading.co.uk
www.calico-moon.co.uk	www.ciel.ltd.uk
www.clothworks.co.uk	www.conkersclothing.co.uk
www.cut4cloth.co.uk	www.eco-eco.co.uk
www.enamore.co.uk	www.eponasport.com
www.equop.com	www.ganesha.co.uk

www.globalkids.co.uk

www.gossypium.co.uk

www.greenfibres.com

www.howies.co.uk

www.naturalcollection.com

www.ralper.co.uk

www.terramar.co.uk

www.thenaturalstore.co.uk

www.traidcraftshop.co.uk

www.glo4life.com

www.greenbaby.co.uk

www.greenknickers.org

www.naturalchild.co.uk

www.peopletree.co.uk

www.seasaltcornwall.co.uk

www.thtc.co.uk

www.toast.co.uk

Health and Beauty

www.caringconsumer.com – US site run by PETA with lots of info on animal testing.

Women's Environmental Network (WEN) have done research into chemicals in cosmetics. **www.wen.org.uk**

Natural toiletries:

www.greenpeople.co.uk

www.spieziaorganics.com

www.essentialcare.co.uk

www.barefootherbs.co.uk

www.nealsyardremedies.com

www.weleda.com

www.akamuti.co.uk

Food:

Big Barn – The Virtual Farmers Market; Tel: 01234 871005, **www.bigbarn.co.uk**

Country Markets Ltd – Tel: 0845 108 3784; **www.country-markets.co.uk**

Divine Chocolate www.divinechocolate.com – fairtrade chocolate producer owned by cocoa farmers' co-operative in Ghana.

The Fairtrade Foundation – Tel: 020 7405 5942; **www.fairtrade.org.uk**

www.fairtrade.net, home to Fairtrade Labelling Association

Friends of the Earth – 'Real Food' campaign **www.foe.co.uk**

Grassroots Action on Food and Farming (GAFF) highlights corporate control of agriculture and builds alliances between environmentalists, campaigners, farmers, farm groups and the public. **www.gaff.org.uk**

International Federation for Alternative Trade (IFAT) www.ifat.org

Local Food Works, www.localfoodworks.org – Web site set up to encourage local and organic food networks, to help shops, cafes, schools, hospitals, prisons, hotels and community centres.

Link Organic, www.linksorganic.com – Directory of organic foods and produce.

National Association of Farmers' Markets – Tel: 0845 4588420; **www.farmersmarkets.net**

Local Exchange Trading Systems (Letslink UK) – Tel: 0207 607 7852; **www.letslinkuk.org**

Soil Association – Tel: 0117 314 5000; **www.soilassociation.org** – Information centre and organic directory on the web site, with details of UK veg box schemes.

Slow Food – Tel: 0800 917 1232; **www.slowfood.com** – Network across 48 countries promoting 'slow food' – quality, local produce. Web site lists UK groups and events.

Viva! Campaigning and researching on the factory farming of animals. Tel: 01273 777688; **www.viva.org.uk**

The **Vegan Society** for information on veganism **www.vegansociety.com**

The **Vegetarian Society** – site packed with information and recipes on all things veggie. Tel: 0161 925 2000; **www.vegsoc.org**

Women's Environmental Network (WEN) – Tel: 020 7481 9004; **www.wen.org.uk/localfood**

WWF – One Planet Living **www.wwf.org.uk/oneplanetliving** – Site that includes details of WWF research into 'ecological footprinting', showing that food is the biggest single factor in the average UK footprint.

Read

Captive State: The Corporate Takeover of Britain George Monbiot (MacMillan)

Shopped! The Shocking Truth about British Supermarkets. Joanna Blythman (Fourth Estate)

Money:

Ethical Investment Research www.eiris.org

www.ethicalinvestment.org.uk, home of the ethical investment association

Ethical Investors Group www.ethicalinvestors.co.uk

Corporate Critic – keep an eye on big business **www.corporatecritic.org**

New Economics Foundation www.neweconomics.org

Cars:

Environmental Transport Association www.eta.co.uk – for green motor insurance, heaps of tips and a green car buyer's guide.

Carsharing is becoming more popular from liftsharing schemes at **www.www.liftshare.com** to car pools at **www.citycarclub.co.uk**.

Find out more about biodiesel at **www.ecobiodiesel.co.uk** or **www.greengoldbiodiesel.co.uk**

Other methods of transport:

www.sustrans.org.uk – the UK's leading sustainable transport charity

www.nationalrail.co.uk – for UK train times

www.seat61.com – for train travel around Europe and beyond.

Travel

If you would prefer not to visit and therefore fund those countries ruled by oppressive regimes, check out **www.amnesty.org** for a current list.

Tourism Concern is an organisation that fights exploitation in tourism. Not against travel; they believe that holidays should be as good for the people in destinations as they are for travellers. See **www.tourismconcern.org.uk**

North South Travel www.northsouthtravel.co.uk; Tel: 01245 608291 – diverts profits into a charitable venture that benefits developing countries by funding grassroots projects.

Responsible Travel www.responsibletravel.com – selects holidays for their ethical credentials. There is a set of criteria and only one in six holiday companies that applies makes the grade.

AITO – The Association of Independent Tour Operators runs its own Responsible Tourism Awards. **www.aito.co.uk;** Tel: 0870 751 8080

Ecotravel can be found at **www.ecotravel.com** with advice on camping gear and travels far afield.

Fairtrade tourism in South Africa is available at **www.fairtourismsa.org.za** or tel: 00 27 12 342 8307. This unique initiative ensures that local people actually benefit from tourism.

Sustainable Tourism Stewardship Council at **www.stscouncil.org**

Tourism and the Environment, Sustaining Scotland's Natural Advantage **www.greentourism.org.uk**

www.planestupid.com is the home of the campaign group against the growth of the aviation industry.

READ:

Ethical Travel Guide: Your passport to alternative holidays
(£12.99 Earthscan)

Green Places to Stay (£13.99 Sawday Publishing)

Alternatives:

The **Anti-Consumerism Campaign** at **www.enough.org.uk**

Buy Nothing Christmas www.buynothingchristmas.org

www.newdream.org New American Dream – useful resources on living a simpler, greener life.

Further Reading:

Magazines:

Ecologist **www.ecologist.com**

Ethical Consumer **www.ethicalconsumer.org**

The Green Parent **www.thegreenparent.co.uk**

Independent News Collective **www.ink.uk.com**

New Consumer **www.newconsumer.com**

New Internationalist **www.newinternationalist.org**

Books:

The toxic consumer (£7.99 Impact Publishing) **www.impactpublishing.co.uk**

Green parenting (£7.99 Impact Publishing) **www.impactpublishing.co.uk**

Life swap (£7.99 Impact Publishing) **www.impactpublishing.co.uk**

Also available from Impact Publishing

The toxic consumer
– How to reduce your exposure to everyday toxic chemicals
The number of man-made chemicals in everyday consumer products is on the increase and it is no longer controversial to claim that many are toxic and compromise our health and yet we are unwittingly and constantly exposed to them.
The Toxic Consumer presents the facts about the chemicals that surround us in our 21st Century lifestyles, and provides easy-to-follow practical advice on how to minimise your exposure.
ISBN: 978 1904601 425   **£7.99**

Green parenting
– Choosing what's best for you, your child and the environment
Lifestyle choices will influence how our children grow up – so what part should the consideration of health issues, organic living and the environment play when we bring up children?
Green Parenting takes you on a practical step-by-step journey from pregnancy through birth and babies, to toddlers and teenagers, offering advice you can act on now. When even small changes can make a big difference to you and your children, this practical guide will prove invaluable.
ISBN: 978 1904601 39 1   **£7.99**

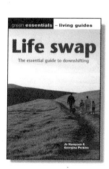

Life swap
– The essential guide to downshifting
Fed up with your current life? Spending too much and enjoying too little? Trapped in a stressful cycle of work and commitments?
Life Swap shows you that there is an alternative – and if you care enough it is achievable. We give you the full low-down on the emotional and financial traps, the psychology for success, the money issues, work/life balance and the trick to changing your habits and expectations.
ISBN: 978 1904601 43 X   **£7.99**

Green Essentials
– organic gardening guides
Practical, fun and each one is focused on just one topic – making it the ideal way for busy gardeners or beginners to get all the top organic tips they need.

£3.99 each

www.impactpublishing.co.uk